The Day My Life Went to the Dogs

How Little Things Make You
Laugh the Hardest

Judy Applefeld

Illustrations by Melanie Fried

The Day My Life Went to the Dogs
Copyright © 2016 by Judith Applefeld

All rights reserved. No part of this book may be reproduced or transmitted in any form or by any means without written permission from the author.

Printed in USA by 48HrBooks (www.48HrBooks.com)

Dedication

This book is dedicated to the memory of my mother, who was willing to go prematurely gray by encouraging me to be the best me I knew how to be;

To Ira, the love of my life, and my friends Dana and Beth, who not only visited the amusement park I live in, but have stayed by my side and even bought tickets for some of the rides;

And lastly but never least to Sarah B, who unknowingly ignited a spark whose light grew bright enough to help me find my way back from a very dark place.

Table of Contents

Introduction

I love animals. I always have. They are smart, warm, silly, loyal, cunning, loving, and above all else, forgiving. I had a friend who was a nun. She and I somehow got on to the topic of euthanasia. I asked why in the world we weren't as kind with suffering people as we were with suffering animals. Her answer floored me. "It's different. Animals have no souls." All I could do was to stare at her in disbelief. Growing up as a good Jewish girl, nuns hold no power over me. I mean no disrespect. It's just that what they wear is no different to me from the uniform of a doctor or pharmacist. I'm not afraid to speak my mind. I reminded her that animals are living, breathing, sentient, feeling beings. She stood firm: "They don't pray." Here the conversation turned a corner. "How do you know they don't pray? Maybe they are thinking the same of us! How do you know that when a car is speeding forward, a squirrel isn't thinking to himself, 'Holy cow! Please, God, get me out of here!'" No matter what I said, she held firmly to her convictions. I'm hoping you'll agree with me that the stories in the book prove her wrong.

Where It All Began

When I was 12 years old, I stopped speaking to my mother for two weeks. Not a word. I refused to be the one to give in. I was on strike. Why? Because I wanted a dog. I had wanted and begged for a dog for as long as I could remember, but always to no avail. I had tried many methods over the years—crying, cajoling, food strikes—you name it. I even went so far as to drag a dog home from a shopping center, trying to convince my mother that it was lost and I could provide the perfect home. He slept in the hall, and I checked on him constantly to prove I was responsible enough to take care of a dog. The next morning, I went to school and came home only to find that the dog I was sure would be mine, actually had the nerve to leave in search of his real home. Not speaking to my mother was a last ditch effort to win the battle. As usual—I lost.

I suppose my attachment to dogs began quite early, without my even realizing it. When I was only six years old, we lived a few doors up from Miss Evelyn, a sweet lady who also seemed to be about my parents' age. Of course from my vantage point, anyone older than high school age fell into the category of about my parent's age. Miss Evelyn lived alone, and was nice enough to the kids, always talking gently, and giving out exceptionally good candy on Halloween. So good in fact, that we would often do a quick change into a second costume and head back to her house a few hours later to collect sweet seconds. We would all gather and examine our treasures, feeling very wise at having completely fooled a grown-up. If Miss Evelyn knew our trick, (and how could she not,) she never let on.

One could never think of Miss Evelyn without thinking of Sweetie. Weighing somewhere between 25 and 35 pounds, Sweetie was the neighborhood dog. She had fairly long black hair that was smooth and silky when brushed, a mid-length slender pointed snout, and a long bushy tail that she always carried high in the air. Sweetie was one of the gang, though instead of joining in our games, she often sat on the sidelines in her yard observing our daily adventures.

Sweetie was never more part of our circle than when the Good Humor man came. Whenever we heard the jingle of his bell, we scattered and disappeared into our homes to get our ice cream money, and then gathered a few moments later along the side of the shiny white truck. We eagerly pointed to the pictures of our chosen delicacy, handed over our twenty-five cents, and retreated to the curb to revel in our delights. But, never until all of us were served, and all of us included Sweetie. Attached to her collar was a small change purse, into which Miss Evelyn would deposit a quarter. After serving us, Mr. Sam would bend down to remove the quarter, and hold out a Dixie cup of vanilla ice cream that Sweetie would gently grab with her teeth. She would come over to the curb with us, and after the paper lid was removed and the cup placed on the ground, Sweetie would sit and eat her afternoon refreshment right along with the rest of us. She may have been a dog, but to us she was surely one of the congregation.

I loved Sweetie about as much as a six-year old can love anything, and a few years later, when we had to move due to the unfortunate circumstance of having our house auctioned out from under us, my tears were more for missing her than any of my human friends. After all, she was always fiercely loyal, never called me names or tried to beat me up. This was far more than I could say about my other friends, especially one boy named Buddy, who lived a few houses down. Thanks to him, I endured so many punches in the nose, that for years it was not unusual for me to wake up to a bloody pillow in the morning.

I was never allowed any pets except goldfish, or those little turtles that always died because their shells got too soft. And then there was the African frog I was allowed to have. It lived in the water like a fish, and was about the size of a half dollar. As with all my pets during my youth, the little guy met his demise way before his time. I had always been in the habit of burying my deceased pets in the back yard. But when the little frog died, I was sick with chicken pox. My mother had thrown me in with all my friends when they had it five months earlier. As would become a lifelong habit of doing everything in my own time, I waited five long months to show the symptoms. Obviously I was too sick to bury my little friend, so I came up with what I thought was an ingenious idea. I laid him in an empty pill box and put him in the freezer until I was well enough to give him his proper send-off. And then I promptly forgot about him—for months. In those days there was no such thing as a self-defrosting freezer. Every three to four months, my mother would empty the freezer and fill it with pots of boiling water to help melt the ice. While the melting was taking place, my mother would go through the things she had removed from the freezer, inspect them, and decide what to keep and what to toss. One afternoon while I was playing in the basement, I heard a blood-curdling scream. Seems she had come across the long ago forgotten pill box. When she lifted the lid, there it was—a frog stiff as a board and laid out like he was ready for a crucifixion. There was no question; I would have to wait years, until I was living on my own, before my fantasy of owning a dog would come true.

Like most post-college youth, I lived in an assortment of different apartments with one or more roommates. Finally, I rented my very own apartment. It came with spiders, a windowsill full of ants, and assorted other uninvited guests that had already taken up residence. I took the apartment anyway, because when I asked the landlord the magic question, "Can I have a dog?" she said yes. Once I heard this magic answer, there was no turning back. I had always assumed my mother wouldn't allow me to have a dog because she didn't like animals. I was about to find out how very wrong I was. Within four months I had my first puppy. And the day I brought her home was, indeed, the day my life went to the dogs.

The World As I See It

Before reading any more of this book, I'd like you to meet a pivotal person who appears throughout the stories...ME! Sharing a little about who I am, and the people in my life, will give you a pretty good idea of how and why I think the way I do. Please allow me these few pages to introduce myself and the small cast of characters who have no doubt shaped who I am.

First you need to know that I've spent a good deal of my life lying down. I'm not talking about sleeping at night or napping during the day—everyone does that. I'm talking about lying down through no choice of my own. I have endured being punched in the nose, falling from trees, plummeting off of scaffolding, and flying out of cars into oncoming traffic, just to mention a few. I've even slammed headfirst into walls. Yes, you read it right...headfirst into a brick wall.

Let me tell you about an incident that happened during my college years, that time of life when young people pretend to be grownups but still need their parents for support in the minor areas of clothing, food, and shelter. On one occasion, we young adults were acting our ages. We were sledding on cafeteria trays, headfirst and backwards down a huge hill that just happened to end at a three-story brick building. While the sledder was enjoying the ride, the friends were at the bottom of the hill, entrusted with the important job of catching the sledder before he or she came crashing into said wall. All was going splendidly until it was my turn, and I noticed I had passed my trusted friends. Not a good sign. Something more important had taken their attention to the top of the hill. I was able to quickly throw my gloved hands over my head which helped somewhat to cushion the blow. But not by much. My gloves were shredded. My back felt like it had been used as an accordion with only one end able to move. My friends came back into service and zoomed me to the emergency room (where I was known on a first name basis.) After much poking, prodding, and scanning, I was sent back to school with horribly sore muscles, but no actual permanent damage. I went through several tubes of Ben Gay. For two weeks I smelled like a wintergreen lifesaver. I couldn't carry a cafeteria tray (with or without food on it) or cut my food. As it turned out this was just practice for a skiing incident a few years later, but that's another story.

I have a history—a long history—of falling off of or out of unbelievable places, only to get back up again. If the truth be told, I have escaped permanent bodily harm or death not only more times than anyone I know, but more times than anyone I know of. I don't just mean during my life as an adult. I'm talking about as far back as I can remember. Not long ago I looked through my yearbook from junior high school. Under my picture, there it was in bold black letters: *"no more broken bones!"* What caught my attention was that this wasn't signed by one of my schoolmates or a teacher. It was written by the school nurse! After enough of these experiences, a person has to somehow be emotionally affected. Some might become strongly religious, feeling their good fortune was held in the hands of a higher power. Some may become serious and philosophical, examining every aspect of cause and effect. And then there are the people who do what I do. I see life from a sideways point of view. I have learned that very little in life should be taken seriously. The bottom line is that my life is never dull. Events in my life take me and everyone who stays with me on a wild ride, never knowing if the direction will be up or down. The only certainty is that if the direction is down, I'd put my money on betting that I fell there.

Now For That Cast of Characters

I spent a long part of my life hoping I was adopted. That was the only possible explanation I could come up with to explain the weirdness of my family. My DNA carries not just addiction and drinking, but also schizophrenia; major and minor retardation; and most of all, rampant stupidity. Think I'm being harsh? Let me briefly share some stories and I'll let you decide.

Most of my family is estranged because so many of them are so... well, strange. I recently began to take notice of the odd array of building material that created and glued together my family. Let's start with one of my cousins. One of my aunts had passed away, and we were all together at his mother's house to be part of the mourning period the Jewish religion calls Shiva. Shiva is the Hebrew word for seven, the number of days of observance. Keeping in tradition with all Mediterranean cultures, there were mounds of food. I say Mediterranean culture not as a way to label any one culture but to show the glaring similarities. Let's look at Jewish, Greek, and Italian families. No meal is considered complete and healthy without at least one appetizer, three or four main courses, and unbelievable desserts. In all three cultures the man is the one in charge and head of the family, but not really. We all know in these families the head honcho is always the mother. And most endearingly, if someone doesn't understand or agree with what you are saying the only way to correct that is to keep talking louder. Surely I'm not the only person to see the uncanny similarity here. But I digress. Back to the story.

One of my favorite cousins was, and still is, one of the most oblivious people I've ever met. My sister was scraping plates in the kitchen to prepare them for washing. She and my cousin stood talking; he was watching her every move as she scraped the leftovers from each plate into the sink drain. After scraping several plates, my sister looked around and inquired where the switch was for the garbage disposal. My cousin's straight faced answer: "We don't have one."   How he makes it through life is a mystery to all of us, as he is like that to this day.

Then there is my beloved niece. We have very close friends who live in Iceland, and many trips have been made back and forth over the ocean. Imagine the look on my face when my then twenty-two year old niece looked at me one day and asked whether it was the sun or the moon you fly over when you go to Iceland. Seeing a thread here?   I won't bore you with more examples. I'm sure you've got the picture.

Don't get me wrong. Many times I've been the first leaf to fall from the tree. I went to college in the Allegany Mountains, three hours away from home. I picked the college because I knew there would be masses of snow. I didn't know the curriculum until I got there. You can see my priorities here. One time, after a week of no sleep and constant studying, I was headed home for a semester break. At one point I stopped to gas up. Now keep in mind, that this is after a series of all-nighters to study or get the paper in that I've had all semester to do but waited until I had real motivation...possibly getting an F in the class. This is the only excuse I can think of for what happened next. The gas attendant looked at me while I waited for the tank to fill, and asked if I'd changed the air in my tires. I told him I didn't think there was any such thing. He just shook his head and said, "That's the problem with you college kids. You get a car, you think you know everything, and you have no idea how to properly service the vehicle." The car was up on the lift before it dawned on me that this guy was playing me for everything he could.

Then there was the time my mother, sister, and I all went to Harpers Ferry for the day. After about an hour I started getting impatient, I asked "Where's the boat?" My mother just looked at me and said "What did you say?" Getting more impatient, I asked again where the heck the boat was. I really thought we were there to ride some ferry boat. I asked one last time where the boat was. My mother didn't miss a beat. She just looked at me while shaking her head, and simply said "Oh sweetheart, I think you missed it." I remember a quote someone once said: "We don't hide our crazy people. We put them right on the front porch." We just seem to have acquired more than our share.

Strange things also happen with the people my family associates with. They seem to pick up our odd family patterns. Take our friend Estelle. She is the mother of two girls who lived down the street from us where I grew up. As I came into adulthood, she and I began interacting not as mother and child, but more as equals. At one time I had discovered a musical artist that I really enjoyed. One day, Estelle, who at the time was a volunteer at a senior center, got in my car and told me how impressed everyone at the center was because I was friends with this musician. There was only one response: "What the heck are you talking about? This person doesn't know I'm a flea on a dog. Where in the world did you get such an idea?" Seems I wasn't clear in presenting myself. One day I had mentioned to Estelle that I had recently been introduced to this artist. I of course, was speaking of being introduced to the music. Estelle took the statement literally, and for months had been telling people that the musician and I were friends. Since then, I've always thought things through once or twice before making any statement that could be misconstrued in any way. Related. Almost related. Sometimes it doesn't matter who the individual is. The best way to summarize it is with a quote by Ethel Mumford: "God gave us relatives...Thank God we can choose our friends."

What helped bolster my high hopes of adoption occurred when my mother was getting ready for major surgery. My family all went down to donate blood. I mean everyone from siblings to nieces and nephews and first and second cousins. What gave me so much hope? Every single person had the same blood type: O positive, except me. I'm A positive. I was sure that was the miracle sign I'd been waiting for. And I felt elated. That is, until someone showed me a photo of my father taken when he was five years old. I held it next to a photo of me at the same age. All hope and elation melted away; the faces were literally identical. So much for those high hopes.

Just for the record, I haven't improved with age one bit. When I first moved into my neighborhood, I found a group of people who walked their dogs at a school close by. One day I was listening to some of the women talking about 'Coach Purses'. For the life of me I couldn't understand why anyone would need a special purse to ride a train.

Crickett's Story

I remember like it was yesterday, clear as a bell; the words repeating over and over in my head: "Don't pick your dog. Let your dog pick you." That was all the information I had to go on. That, and that I knew I wanted a female puppy. So off we went, my sister and me, to get my first ever dog. My new best friend. A friend I had been asking for and praying for my whole life. Little did I know how completely my life was about to change.

The night before I brought my little girl home I cleaned like a woman possessed. For the first time, I looked at everything from a six-inch level. The first thing I noticed was that I was an even worse house keeper than I gave myself credit for. And on a scale of one to ten, I had already listed myself in the minus column. So armed with gloves, cleansers, a bucket and rags, I began to tackle every square inch of anything that I feared would be within puppy reach and could possibly cause my soon to be daughter harm. It was an evening of constant discovery. Imagine my surprise as I discovered the true color of my floor, baseboards, and walls! Not to mention the collection of lost coins, jewelry, pens, and a wide assortment of other treasures.

I had no idea that the length of time it takes to clean is proportional to the amount of years the build-up had been allowed to populate. In simpler terms, it took forever! But I had a purpose—a goal. And so I persevered. I have no idea how many families ranging from the small to the microscopic I evicted that evening. It wasn't until later that I discovered there was a small family of mice living in the house with me that never did move out, but we did learn to cohabitate together. I slept that night feeling both contentment in knowing I had achieved such a major accomplishment, and excitement in knowing that tomorrow I would meet my new daughter.

I remember it was a Friday evening. I wanted the weekend to be able to stay home and help my little one adapt to her new surroundings. Actually that's a lie. I knew I'd be too excited to sleep, and I wanted as much time as possible to play and fall in love with my new treasure. So there I stood, looking at seven balls of fluff. Only four were females. Of those four I picked each one up and held them close. One whined and cried. One burped. One just stared at me like she was trying to cast a spell. Then I picked up the last one, and she immediately licked my face. But I didn't want to be hasty. So I went through the same routine a few more times. And sure enough, every time I picked her up she licked my face. It was fate—Kismet! Love at first sight. I had done as I was told and let my dog pick me. It wasn't until I got her home and we started to settle in together that I realized she picked me because she was the one smart enough to see the words "easy target" on my forehead. She was six weeks old and small enough to fit in one hand. I wasn't sure what to name her. After meeting her and seeing the wet spots on the floor, my brother-in-law suggested the name Puddles. But I had always had a certain name in mind for my first dog...Crickett.

The house Crickett had lived in was, well, rank. It was eventually condemned by the health department. Maybe all those kisses were her being grateful to be rescued. She was the cutest thing I'd ever seen, shiny black hair with tan markings on her face and her feet. And she was also the worst smelling creature I'd ever encountered. We went from the car immediately to the bathroom, and Crickett had her first bath. She patiently sat in the tub while we bathed her. I thought she was grateful to have someone care enough to make sure she was clean. I would later learn that wasn't the case at all. What I mistook for patience was really expectation. Why shouldn't I treat her like royalty? After all, I soon learned, she thought herself quite the little queen! I'm sure, had she been more human, she would have held her paw out to me expecting a pedicure. I learned something else from that first bathing experience. Simply put, *never* bathe a dog without wearing raingear.

As I said, because she was small enough to fit in one hand, her first bed was a shoebox. Honest! It was only for a few nights, but she really slept in a shoebox with a towel in it. I didn't sleep all night that first night. Every time I heard her little feet patter on the wooden floor I immediately jumped up and took her outside. I had the smartest dog in the universe. I was sure she would be housetrained by the time she was seven weeks old. And sure enough, by her seventh week of life, housetraining had happened...to me. By the end of the first week I knew just when to jump and carry her out to the yard-- after every meal, every drink of water, every treat, and every 15 minutes in between just for good measure. It didn't help any that Crickett was...well...short. She learned to sit in just two days. Unfortunately, her little bottom was so close to the ground I couldn't tell a sit from a squat.   She was however, very good at following the rules. Whenever she had to go, she would sit by the door and not make a sound. If I didn't respond quickly enough, I had an extra mess on my hands to deal with. I never got angry. After all she was upholding her end of the bargain! And so every time she tried to sit comfortably, I'd swoop her up and take her outside. I spent so much time carrying her outside I think she was probably three months old before she even knew how to walk on her own!

I guessed it would take several weeks for Crickett and me to learn about each other, to get used to each other, and to become a team. Again I was wrong. I had greatly misjudged the situation. Crickett showed her true personality right away. We often took morning walks together. Many of our friends walked at this time, but I always made a point of walking in the opposite direction. I had a cup of coffee in one hand, a leash in the other, and wore a sweatshirt that summed up my personality. On the back in four-inch high letters were three simple words. Crickett was clearly cut from the same spirit and pattern as was I. Though invisible to the naked untrained eye, she also was wearing a sweatshirt whose message was equally as succinct. Where mine said LEAVE ME ALONE, hers simply said ME TOO.

When Crickett was barely seven weeks old, I took her to visit her "grandma". Now remember, this was the woman who for years had refused to let me have a dog. The two of us walked into my mother's apartment and immediately got hit in the face with this amazing aroma. We both stopped in our tracks, noses in the air, sniffing as though the actual taste would just pour into our mouths. I asked, "What is that?" My mother's response: "Don't you dare touch that! Its beef stew. I made it for the baby." There it sat, totally out of my reach. A pot of beef stew with small beef cubes, carrots, potatoes, peas, gravy, and assorted spices. So much for my mother's not liking animals. Not only did she love them; she adored them—at least her granddog. It wasn't until years later that I would learn the reason for her aversion to my having a pet while growing up. For right now, it was a match made in heaven. Sure enough, the baby got the goods; I got spaghetti. This was the beginning of my realizing the harsh reality of all new pet owners. No matter what you read and how hard you work at it, you are at best a co-leader of your pack.

What began here was an interesting trend that took me years to catch on to. Anytime my mother would babysit, Crickett was allowed to eat to her heart's delight. I wasn't there to monitor, so there was no judging how much, or what she ate. She loved to visit her Grandma. But sure enough, every time we got home, she threw up. I once mentioned to a friend that I was amazed Crickett wasn't more afraid to visit my mother. My friend set me straight. "She eats whatever she wants at your mother's. I'm amazed she isn't afraid to come home. That's where she gets sick!"

I think my mother found a kindred spirit in Crickett that she just couldn't find with me, because I'm more selective about what goes into my mouth. I don't do gooey very well. I don't care for cream or jelly filled pastries, whipped cream, milkshakes, sweet sauces, or anything that disappears before I chew it. Unfortunately, my mother made it difficult to feed my little girl at home. I would put down her regular food and she would sit there glaring at me. If she could have talked, there is no doubt in my mind she was clearly saying, "What the heck is this? Call the manager. I ordered steak!"

A prime example of my tastes versus Crickett's, would be when I had a friend over for dinner one evening. She brought what she thought would be the perfect dessert—a Napoleon. Perfect for many people but not for me. After dinner, my friend and I went into the living room to visit, leaving the Napoleon in the middle of the kitchen table. Crickett was about three months old at this point and had not yet made great strides in the height department. About an hour later, my friend and I went back into the kitchen to discover there was no longer any dessert at all. My little furry child was showing the beginnings of outsmarting me. She had pushed a chair closer to the table, jumped up on the chair, and made one more leap onto the table. There she sat in the middle of the table happily licking the paper the dessert had been in. Did she seem at all sorry? NO! When we entered the room she just stood up, looked at me with a very satisfied expression on her face while her tail wagged high in the air.

Her tricks with food didn't stop with desserts. When we visited Grandma, Crickett always got a handful of small dog cookies. She went into "hide the cookie" mode right away. First, she tried to bury them next to a large stereo speaker in the living room. She put the cookies down next to the speaker and proceeded to cover them with nothing but air. It was really funny to watch her moving absolutely nothing with her nose to cover the cookies. The best part was the surprised look on her face when she stepped back and realized her treasures were still in plain view for everyone to see. But she was nothing if not determined. Later in the day, my mother and I started looking for the treats to see where Crickett may have finally put them. Seeing nothing we just assumed she had eaten them. That is until my mother started to pull her bedspread down for the evening. Six perfect cookies came flying out from where the spread was tucked under the pillows. That was another lesson learned; we had no idea she was tall enough to jump onto the bed.

My little girl proved to be way ahead of herself very quickly. For the first few weeks, I left her in a little area in the kitchen closed off with a baby gate. I was working nearby and would stop in during my lunch break to get her outside and be sure she was doing ok. Less than two weeks later, I came home to find all of my laundry scattered over the living room floor. What the heck? I gently put Crickett behind the baby gate, sat in a chair, and just waited. It didn't take 60 seconds before she climbed up the mesh of the gate and simply dropped herself over on the other side. I'd had her less than two weeks and she was already outsmarting me at every turn.

In no time, Crickett was my constant companion. Those first few months riding in the car were priceless. She was so short that when she stood on her hind legs, she still couldn't reach the bottom of the passenger door window. We went everywhere together. I never wanted human children; I was wise enough to know that, but I was to discover that either way many new parenting lessons were still to come.

Crickett taught me everything I know about being a doggie parent. As with any child, the most caution is taken with the first. And so it was here. I came to understand all of her sounds and looks. Whether I paid heed to them is something else. At one time I was an amateur photographer. I was experimenting taking portrait pictures using only candles for lighting. Any of you who are familiar with photography in the old days (boy, writing THAT hurts) know that all aperture settings had to be set by hand, along with shutter speed. As with many things, the old-fashioned way takes longer but gives more satisfying results. The whole time this is going on, Crickett is sitting on the bed looking at me and making that low growling sound that meant "I need to go, please." Her growls became louder and more insistent, but I kept saying, "Hold on Crickett, just one more minute." Those minutes added up more quickly than I realized, and Crickett was at the end of her patience. And so, true to her form, she barked once, glared right at me...and peed on the bed. Not a hint of remorse. Just two eyes staring at me, leaving no question what she was thinking. "I *told* you I had to go! Don't blame *me*. And *don't* do it again!" Lesson learned, and one mattress heavily cleaned—and flipped over.

That of course isn't all she taught me. I don't mean to ruin anyone's appetite, but let's face it—nobody likes to throw up. Out of respect for my readers, I won't use that graphic wording again. Bottom line is that no one likes that feeling. No matter how old I get, as soon as I feel that feeling, I want my mother. Now, I had to view everything from a different perspective: I was the mother. The problem was that being a human with no canine experience, I had no idea whatsoever what to look for. Mothers wore towels when holding infants because there was never any warning of what was to come. As the children got older, mothers knew, because a child could tell them something was amiss.

Dogs—that's a whole other story. The way I found that out was, well, both surprising and endearing. At the time, I was unaware of the complications that can come from changing from one dog food to another cold-turkey rather than gradually. I found out the dangers the hard way. I saw a commercial for a new soft and chewy food with beef and cheese all mixed together. It looked like the kind of thing a dog would like, so I bought some, gave it to Crickett for dinner and never gave it another thought. I sure wish I had known more then.

A few hours later I was in bed propped up and reading, with my little angel on the bed with me. Suddenly she started whining and walking around in a circle. Silly me–I thought she had to go out. By then she knew what it meant if I asked if she had to go out, and always reacted if she had to, or lay down if she didn't. When I asked this time, she did neither; she just kept whining and circling. She walked over and stood on my lap. I tried to comfort her by putting my hand out to pet her or hold her. Big mistake. She stared at me, made this strange noise like a pump about to break, and got sick—all over the front of me and the bedding. Ugh! Now instead of relaxing I had work to do. Off with the sheets and T-shirt and downstairs into the laundry. Then into the shower for both of us. Finally, came new bed linens and clean clothes. It was a lesson I would never forget. After that and throughout my life whenever I hear that sound, I throw newspaper down as quickly as I can and move as far away as possible. It was a long time before she was sick again, and for some reason from then on she made my work easy for me by always going to the same spot: the mat on the bathroom floor. I was never sure if she decided to do that to make my life easier or if it just became a habit. Either way, I was always very grateful.

Crickett left many a heart pounding with anxiety and fear on more than one occasion. And for some reason, she had one particular person that she liked to scare most often. I will never forget the first time she left Harriette's heart fibrillating. My mom was scheduled to go into heart surgery the following day. Harriette, our trusty next door neighbor and practically a relative, had offered to take Crickett for a walk with her canine daughter Ariel. All was fine, or so I thought. After a few moments, my upstairs neighbor Sharon, came knocking on my door. "Do you know where Crickett is?" "Of course", I answered. She went for a walk with Harriette. "I wouldn't be so sure", said Sharon. "She's in the front yard without a tether and looking very proud of herself." I went to look for myself, and sure enough there was Crickett standing in the yard alone and looking very full of herself. "What the...?" I murmured, when suddenly I saw Harriette running as fast as she could down the street. She got to the yard, panting so hard she could barely get her words out. "I got up to the school and let Crickett off her leash. That quick, she turned tail and in that 'I'm gonna trot just quickly enough that you can't catch me' move, she started speed walking home. I ran and yelled and yelled and ran, and she stayed just out of my reach!"

Now I had diligently worked with Crickett to teach her to sit at every curb before walking into the street. So naturally my next question was "Did she at least sit at the curb?" "Oh yes," was the answer. "She sat every time." Feeling very proud, I said "Really? That's great! How long did she sit?" The answer: "About a second!" "Oh," I said. Harriette, still wheezing and gasping, and with a look in her eye I'd never seen before, summed up the experience. "As soon as I took off the leash she booked. I ran and yelled, and the louder I yelled the faster she trotted". By now she was spitting out her words in a very measured cadence; one word for every breath. Through clenched teeth she said, "I couldn't decide if I should be nervous or REALLY PISSED OFF!" It was then that I realized I had successfully taught my little girl how to sit before going into the street. Unfortunately, I had forgotten to teach her why. Her sitting for only a second or two told me that she had no idea *why* she was sitting. She had no clue what traffic was, nor did it register that it was something to be cautious about. Sitting at the curb, for Crickett, was simply a game I had taught her. Oh well...I tried.

You would think that horrific incident would be enough to last a lifetime. Not so. When Crickett was about six years old, a very close friend lay dying in the hospital. My trusty next door neighbor had moved, and she was the only one I could count on in a doggie emergency. I knew my hours at the hospital would be long and erratic. Rather than relying on the kindness of strangers, I sent Crickett to stay with Harriette. All was fine until 8:00 one morning. Those were the days of pagers, not cell phones. My pager began beeping and I immediately recognized the number. I called Harriette only to hear the words "Crickett ran away. She's looking for you." I don't know how many of you remember the 'Keep on Truckin' guy from the early seventies. It was a cartoon of a shlumpy looking guy with one foot stretched way ahead of the other. Those of you who do indeed remember it will understand what I'm about to say. My friend was on the sixth floor of the hospital.

When I got the message about Crickett, I ran immediately to my car. I went down six flights taking at least four steps at a time. As I got in my car, I got the message that Crickett had found her way back to my friend, but already being on a roll, I zoomed back to the house to comfort my little girl. I should have known better. No matter what the crisis, Crickett was still Crickett. I ran into the house and found Harriette holding my bundle of joy just like a human baby, head over the human shoulder. I went up to her face to see and comfort her. And what did she do??? She looked every place but at me. No matter how I positioned myself, Crickett made it clear my infraction was unforgivable and refused to look at me. I was extremely elated that she was safe and sound, but after her reception all I could hear myself saying was "I can't believe I am suffering major shin splints for this." I limped painfully for more than a week. But Crickett didn't bat an eye.

Of course she also made sure that I had my share of being scared to death. We used to walk the track of an abandoned high school. We went every day at the same time. Crickett had her friends, I had mine. I paid little attention to her comings and goings because she always stayed in sight. Well, almost always. One particular day when it was time to go home, I looked around for her and she was nowhere to be found. I didn't panic right away. My friend and I redid an entire lap. Surely she would turn up. But no, she continued to elude us. The longer we searched, the more I panicked. On my third trip around I saw it. Fleeting. Almost imperceptible. Something caught my eye. A flash, a glint. I walked closer, looking harder. And then I saw it clearly. A pair of eyes staring at me from behind a bush. She had been watching us circle and call for her for almost 20 minutes. Anyone who has really loved someone who couldn't be found or reached for one reason or another and suddenly showed up with some ridiculous excuse will be familiar with the mood shift. It went from "Oh please let her be ok" to "I want to smack you silly." Relief has a strange effect on people. This experience was the closest to the fear my poor mother endured when I would wander off and she couldn't find me.

The world was very different when I was a child. There was no fear of a child being harmed or kidnapped. We had free rein to wander where we pleased...within reason. Of course, what a parent found reasonable compared to the child were two completely different things. Things are very different now. Today if a child is injured playing on a pile of rocks around a construction area the, contracting company gets sued. When I was little we were punished for wandering into such a dangerous place. Got a bad scratch or cut? No problem-here's the Bactine and a band aid. It serves you right for not thinking or paying attention.

I'd like to say I was a good teacher for Crickett, but if the truth be told she was the one who patiently and not so patiently taught me. It was she who brought out my first touch of feeling maternal. When she was still quite young, she had a small growth removed. Fortunately, it turned out to be nothing. When I picked her up from the vet later that afternoon, it was clear she was still feeling the glorious effects of the anesthesia. Her eyes were dilated and even though she was no doubt glad to see me, she couldn't quite focus. Between her eyes and the staggering walk of a drunken sailor, if I hadn't known better I'd have sworn she had indeed had a pint or two. I went directly from the vet to visit my mother. I carried my little girl up the steps to my mom's apartment and gently placed her on the carpet. I thought she would just curl up and sleep it off. Nope! She sat staring up at me the entire time letting out a pathetic whimper. That's when the feeling of mommy-hood hit me. I picked her up, lay back on the sofa, and just laid her on me. In less than 30 seconds she was fast asleep.

Just a few words for anyone reading this who actually thinks pets are better than human kids because they can't talk back—let's just say if this were a true or false question and your answer is true, then I have to say you are a bit, shall we say, clueless. I mean no disrespect, but anyone with a vocal pet, be it feline, avian, or canine, knows damn well that not only do they talk back but they almost always win the argument. One morning, I was trying to get Crickett into the house so I could leave for work. She had no intention of doing any such thing. Thus began the battle of the wills. I would try to get her up the steps and she would growl and throw in a few barks. This went on for several minutes. Suddenly I heard my neighbor's voice. I didn't realize she had witnessed the whole thing. She simply looked at me and asked "Is it me or did that dog just cuss you out?"

My all-time favorite story about Crickett having a mind of her own is the time I had the flu. I very rarely get sick, but this really did me in. Any movement at all made me queasy. Because she was so accustomed to sleeping on the bed, (I'm sorry. I meant to say I was used to her letting me into the bed,) she had no desire to be any place else. My poor stomach couldn't take it. I asked her to get down. She glared at me and grumbled under her breath, but refused to move. I again asked her to get off the bed, this time trying to sound like I was the one in charge. Her response was no different. Finally, with what little strength I could gather, I forced her off the bed. She didn't go quietly. She walked to the edge of the bed, growled and glared at me. Finally, she jumped off the bed, walked to the door to the bedroom, and I kid you not, she turned around, teeth bared, growling and glaring, and finally turned and left the room. All of that effort, just so I could sleep undisturbed in my own bed.

A common thread that runs through my family is how well we handle crisis situations. Either we overreact or pretend to have not been aware of the situation. Let me share my mother's reaction when she found out she was pregnant with me. For the times I was a very late in life baby. Today it isn't at all uncommon for women to have their first child in their late thirties. The norm the decade I was born into was very much the opposite: 37 was considered very late indeed. When the doctor called to give my mother the news, she acted exactly as expected. The conversation went something like this: "Minnie, it's Dr. Radman. I have some news for you." "Really? What news?" "The rabbit died." "Oh my God, that's terrible! Which Rabbi?"

Then there was my Aunt Flo. She wasn't really an aunt, but I never thought of her as anything but. In my-mid 30's I had a good friend who entrusted me with knowing that she was an incest survivor. I wanted to support her but had no idea how. I quickly learned that the only way to learn how to offer support was to pay for my own counseling session, an answer I found absurd. Had she been an alcoholic, I could have gone to Al Anon. If she abused drugs, there was Nar Anon. So I decided to take action and form a support group for people in my position. I found someone to help me by giving us a large room in her building to hold meetings. I had another friend print up brochures. The biggest step was getting the word out. I contacted an endless number of social workers, psychologists, and psychiatrists. The next step was doing as much PR as possible. Articles and interviews with me were printed everywhere in every paper and magazine that was willing to help. Sure enough, Aunt Flo's daughter saw one of the articles and shared the information with her mother. "Mom, I just read an interesting article about Judy. She's starting a support group for people who are supporting incest survivors." True to form, Aunt Flo's reaction couldn't have been more perfect. "A group about insects!!! What kind of insects?"

My furry friends seem to have picked up on this irrational behavior to perfectly small situations. I used to take Crickett with me when I was painting someone's house. One day, I was working at the house of someone who owned a particularly large cat. All of her furniture was very low to the ground. Even the night tables were at eye level if I was low on my knees. One day Crickett chased this twenty-five pound cat under the bed. Feeling very proud and full of herself, she turned to me to share the moment. As she was turning towards me, she came face to face with a ceramic cat sitting on a very low night table. Her first reaction was to gasp and stare at this large cat that, in her mind, she had just chased under the bed. Her eyes became huge, her hair stood up, and she started barking louder and more frantically than I had ever witnessed before or since. It was as though she was yelling at this cat saying "Where in the heck did you come from? I just chased you under the bed! Who do you think you are? You get right back where you belong!" I finally had to pull my poor unbalanced baby away from the night table by holding her close and saying over and over, "Crickett please calm down. You're embarrassing yourself."

Crickett also possessed the same luck as I have in regard to walking away from what could have killed me. One evening we were walking along the sidewalk, when potential disaster struck. It was late at night. Crickett had black fur with some markings in tan. Two young men were walking behind us when all hell broke loose. They didn't initially see each other because it was so dark. Suddenly they came across each other. Startled, Crickett barked, frightening one of the young men to react by kicking in her direction. The problem? Crickett's reaction was to run—into the street. At the very same moment, a car was barreling down the street. It happened very quickly. Crickett ran into the street just as a car was zooming by. I was terrified. Fortunately, she had her mother's luck. She did not get hit by the car, but she took off and ran to the yard in back of the house. I found her a minute or two later, shaking all over, but otherwise in perfect shape. Now tell me that doesn't sound like somehow she got my "nothing can really harm me" genes.

What was so amazing about this little girl was her stamina. When she was thirteen, she slid on some ice and tore her cruciate, which is a ligament in the knee. It's a very common and very painful injury in dogs. It requires major surgery, lots of bed rest and a long recovery. The hardest part was keeping her from chewing and licking the area. We tried everything. Then I kid you not—I found the answer in a dream. Off I went to the store to buy her a onesie like the kind babies wear. It was perfect. It covered all four legs, and the snaps were behind her rear legs. I left a hole for her tail to stick out, and whenever she had to go to the bathroom I simply unsnapped those snaps. I recommend this to anyone who needs to keep an area safe but doesn't want to put a cone around the neck.

As I've mentioned, Crickett's face was very emotional. Never did I see it more than when I put this garment on her. She sat on the living room chair glaring at me with pronounced disgust. I'm not sure she ever forgave me for that. My favorite memory was as she was healing and walking. In the beginning there were small walks with lots of limping. As time went on, the limp was less and less pronounced until it was almost gone. I say almost because my little girl held it in reserve for sympathy. She would be walking behind me perfectly fine. That is, until I would look around to see how she was doing. Like any kid, as soon as she caught me looking, the limp returned. I can tell you she played that limp with people for all it was worth.

Even more amazing is what happened when she was sixteen. She had gone on a painting job with me, and at one point we opened the storm door to go outside to take a break. As with many storm doors, this particular one never closed quickly. Instead, it closed in small intervals until the latch finally caught. The customer and I assumed Crickett had come in with us. Alas, an hour later when I went to find her, she was nowhere to be found. I looked all around outside and still no Crickett. I was really getting concerned. I called one of the people who walked with our group and she came over with her do, hoping that would help. We even spoke to a city workman about the problem. That wonderful man opened every manhole cover within a three square block area to look and listen in case she had fallen in a drain. Still no Crickett. I called all of the vets close to the area. An hour became almost two when I suddenly got a call.

Another of our dog walking friends was on her way home, when she noticed the van in front of her moving really slowly. She realized he was following something. When she strained her head she saw that it was Crickett. Obviously someone or something was looking out for her. My friend ran to get her, but Crickett was too fast to catch. The gentleman in the van asked if she was a biter. When my friend answered no, he jumped into action. With his long legs, he just loped until he passed her and grabbed. My friend took Crickett to her home and immediately called me. Not only had she crossed one very busy road once, she crossed another one at least twice. This little girl had run almost a mile and was caught just before the entrance and exit ramps to the Beltway! What were the odds that, of all people, she was found by someone who knew her? I zoomed to my friend's house, ran to the basement, and found Crickett running back and forth, totally discombobulated. She was even running from me. I was able to grab her and it took her a moment to orient herself and realize I had her and she was safe. Don't tell me miracles don't happen.

Along Came Mandy

When Crickett was 10, we had an unexpected visitor that stopped by and never left. I had just come out of the house with Crickett to take her for her daily constitutional. Across the street, I saw a very skinny dog slowly limping on three legs. I crossed the street to get her, and she immediately hid under a parked car. I waited a while, and sure enough she crawled out and resumed her journey along the sidewalk. Once again I tried to approach, but this time, through no fault of her own, she trapped herself in the corner of a fence. I slowly put the back of my hand out for her to sniff. She was timid, leery, and scared. But after a few sniffs, she licked the back of my hand and I knew I had won that silent argument. I wrapped a leash around her neck, took her back to my house, and immediately put her in the car and headed off to the vet. The way she acted in the waiting room should have been my first clue. All twenty-five pounds of her quietly sat in my lap—until another dog walked in. She immediately went from docile to barking her head off. In dog language it was clear she was saying, "Back off buddy, this one is mine. I found her first!" After much poking, prodding, and x-rays, it was determined that this little nine month old dog had been hit by a car and skidded across the street. The result was a badly injured side and a fractured pelvis.

When I first told my Mom about Mandy, she read me the riot act. I heard all about my not being able to afford two dogs; how I wouldn't be allowed to visit her with two dogs; how Crickett would be miserable with another dog in the house. For the first several weeks it was bed rest only. Mandy wasn't allowed to travel. My mom had to come to me so we could visit. Once again my mother showed her true colors. She walked in the door, and the first thing she said was "Mandy, I'm your grandma, you just don't know me yet." Then she handed me a paper bag. I asked her what was in the bag. It was a heating pad for the baby, in case she needed it to feel more comfortable. So much for her not wanting me to have two dogs. Like me, she thought of them as smaller furry people. Not once did she ask about a visit to the vet. It was always "What did the pediatrician say?" I even came home to voice mails where she spoke directly to them. I wish I had saved my favorite one. It was a long rambling message for me about something or other, and just as I thought the message was over, there was a pause, and I heard my mother saying "Mandy, are you on the sofa? You better get off that sofa before your mother comes home and catches you!"

Every parent has one child that stands out as needing extra love and patience. Of all my pets, Mandy should have come with a book of instructions. She was a problem child from the beginning. From day one she was a challenge and a handful. I didn't know her background, but whatever she had been through left her very nervous and frightened. She was a non-

41

stop barker. I lived in an apartment on the first floor of a house. The poor woman who lived above us couldn't cross her own living room without Mandy going on a barking binge. Any loud noise or new person would set her off. My poor mother would go into the bathroom, but Mandy would stand outside the door barking her head off with no intention of letting my mother out.

Somehow, this erratic behavior reminded me of myself at a young age. According to my mother, I also started out as a problem child. While I don't remember the incident, my mother was called to the principal's office when I was, are you ready— in kindergarten. Finger painting was very popular in those days. Obviously paper art bored me, so I opted for something a little more out of the box. I painted one of my classmates from head to toe with the finger paint. I can't begin to imagine what it must have been like for my poor mother to be told her five-year old had the makings of a juvenile delinquent.

Non-stop barking was the least of the problems that came with this little girl. She was starving when I found her; she weighed in at 25 pounds, and would grow to be 50 pounds— quite a difference. Because her system was so compromised, it was difficult for her to keep her food down. For the first few months she threw up every time she ate. After three or four months, she could hold her food down unless she was nervous or frightened, which more or less still left me cleaning up several times a week. Slowly she regained her weight and became the beauty she was meant to be.

Thanks to her nerves, her need to destroy was never ending. One of my favorite stories is about the library book. She ate it—literally. I had to call the library and explain what had happened and to find out the cost to replace the book. I suddenly felt like I was 12 years old, telling my teacher my dog had eaten my homework. Among the long list of items ruined were two pillows, one ink pen (you can imagine what that looked like), and both sides of the mattress. But the number one prize goes to eating the book the trainer had loaned me so I could learn how to keep her calm and prevent her from chewing things.

A close second prize goes to her total destruction of a metal crate. Less than a year after Mandy came to live with us, I moved into my very own house. It is a wonderful older house with a large fenced-in yard for playing. Finally, a home where I could do anything I wanted. The day of the move, I took Mandy to stay with my sister in the pet shop she owned at the time. The move itself took several hours packing and unpacking a rented moving van. In total, Mandy was with my sister about six hours or so. Unfortunately, that proved to be five hours and fifty-nine minutes too long. True to form, my little angel went berserk the minute I walked out of the shop. She immediately began barking, yelping, and thrashing—anything to escape her metal prison. When I finally returned she was exhausted and resting comfortably. The crate, however, was a total loss. Bars were bent on all sides and the top. So much that we had to do major manipulating to get the door open. Never before or since have I ever seen a metal crate so totally demolished—not to mention my sister's nerves.

As I said earlier, when dealing with any problem child, patience is a beautiful necessity. Mandy was a shining star of proof. Not only did we go to obedience class, the trainer took a special interest in her and would stop by my home for free lessons. At one point she informed me that she didn't think Mandy would ever be a social animal. Endless patience proved her wrong. A year later my little girl and I went back to school for a refresher. The very same trainer, who a year ago said my chances of having a stable dog were iffy at best, now pointed Mandy out as a star pupil. Her exact words to the rest of the class were "The changes that I see in this dog are monumental," and she used Mandy as the ultimate example of time and patience. Allow me to add very strong nerves.

Testing to see when she was ready to be left out of her crate when I wasn't home brought lots of laughs--and danger. The first time I was only gone for half an hour. I got a frantic call from the woman living on the second floor. I better get home right away. The smoke alarm was going off and Mandy wouldn't let her in the apartment. I was home in a matter of minutes. There she stood at the doorway, smiling and wagging her tail as if nothing were wrong. I followed a strange smell into the kitchen and was horrified to see a flame burning under the pan I had used to make breakfast. The stove was very old; probably as old as the house. The knobs were on the front, and unlike today's stoves, you didn't need to push the knobs in to turn them. Even without being there, I knew exactly what had happened. Celebrating her new found freedom, Mandy tried to explore everything, including the stove top. She rose on her hind legs to look, and turned a knob with her paw on the way down. No doubt that was the most harrowing experience I can ever remember with all of my dogs.

That experiment was clearly a flop, so I waited a few weeks and tried again. Getting out of my car when I returned, I saw the exterminator standing on the walkway to the house. I asked him if he was just arriving or leaving, desperately hoping for the former. But no; he was leaving. I asked if he was ok with Mandy. He said she barked a lot, but didn't bother him. "Seems kinda nervous though," were the last words I heard. I zoomed in, not knowing what I would find, but I knew it would be something. And so it was; she had chewed a hole through the sheets and mattress the size of a dinner plate. I did the only thing I could do. I covered the hole with trusty duct tape and flipped the mattress over.

A few weeks later I tried again. I've long since become a vegetarian (more about that later) but at that time, I was defrosting chops for dinner. I was accustomed to having a dog Crickett's size, but Mandy was bigger and taller. I began to prepare dinner only to realize there was no dinner to prepare-the chops were both gone, nowhere to be found. All that remained was the empty plate they had been sitting on. Eventually, I saw the remains of one. But where in the world was the other one? I looked everywhere I could think of, and finally gave up, assuming she had eaten the other one, bone and all. Imagine my surprise later that evening to find it in the back of my closet behind the shoes. Whether she hid it in haste to avoid being caught, or just buried it for later is a question that will never be answered.

As I've mentioned, Mandy had a very complicated ego. She was very alpha—in the house. Outside of the house she could have been the smallest dog on the planet. Everything frightened her. She was afraid of people, loud noises, other dogs, and her shadow, just to name a few. After a month or two of her recovery, I would take her and Crickett to a park not far from where we were living. It had a great winding, twisting paved path that meandered through the entire park. The foliage was bountiful and beautiful. And impossible to see through. One day we were walking along the path with some friends when, oh my God, there was a monster of a dog barking and snarling at my baby. When I say a monster of a dog, I mean all of about 20 pounds. This compared to Mandy's 50 pounds. Of course you can see where Mandy would have been at a disadvantage. This little tiger of a dog came up on us unexpectedly, and Mandy being her strong, assertive self took off like a bat out of hell. Away from me. On a very winding path. Where I couldn't possibly keep her in sight. Off I ran like the mother bat chasing the bat out of hell, screaming her name and praying she hadn't taken off, never to be found. Fortune was on my side. A minute or two later, just as my side was hurting and my breathing labored, I saw Mandy barreling toward me at top speed with her eyes wide as saucers and her ears plastered back on her head. I didn't know if I should laugh or cry. She came back and I was thrilled. She had been spooked by a dog one-third her size. Now that's just sad. But she wouldn't remain a coward for too long.

As with Crickett, I took Mandy to a nearby school to walk and learn to socialize. For a long time, she was afraid to let anyone near her. Her best friend was a boxer named Georgia. The two of them became fast friends. It was almost like they were fused together. They would run back and forth up and down the football field. Mandy holding on to Georgia's cheek, Georgia hanging on to Mandy's tail. Every once in a while, they would change the script, both grab a stick at each end, and mow down anything or anyone foolish enough to get in their way. One fine day, we were at the school when a larger shepherd type dog showed up. As expected, Mandy turned tail and ran to me. But something must have exploded in her brain. She stopped a few feet in front of me and seemed to, for just a second, hesitate like she was considering the situation. She turned around, and ran top speed toward the dog she had just run from. And scared that dog to death. The whole field broke into applause and shouts of "Go Mandy go!"

Until she really became sure of herself, she would practice being a bully at home. She would find any reason at all to fight with Crickett. Even though she was smaller of stature, Crickett was not one to back down. This was the birth of my learning how to avoid or break up dog fights. My favorite memory is of a day I took both of them to visit my sister, who had three dogs and at least seven cats (which leads to a whole other story). Crickett and Mandy literally spent the entire three hours lying side by side hiding under the dining room table. On the ride home they stuck close together. That time of peace only lasted until we got home. As soon as we crossed the threshold into the house, Mandy went through some sort of metamorphosis. She turned into Rosemary's baby. Within less than five seconds she turned around and tried to beat the crap out of Crickett. Anything to save face.

I also learned how different one dog can be from another. Thinking what was ok for one dog was also ok for another was a big mistake. I took Crickett everywhere with me. If it was a nice day and I was only going to be a few minutes, I would keep the car windows down so she could catch the breeze and she would just stretch out and bask in the sun. Foolishly, I assumed that I could do the same with Mandy, especially since she had Crickett in the car to watch and learn from. One beautiful day I drove over to the grocery store with my trusty companions in tow. I only needed five items. I was in the store for less than four minutes. I was standing in line, the next to be checked out, when I heard an announcement: "Will the person who had a dog tied up outside please go to the parking lot. Your dog is running around loose." Immediately I knew. There was no question. Mandy had jumped out of the car and was wandering around the parking lot looking for me. There was only one thing I could do. I put my basket of only five items down and went outside. Sure enough, all the way down the parking lot a good Samaritan was standing on the sidewalk holding Mandy's leash. As soon as she saw me, she ran to me. I thanked the woman for taking such good care of my baby, put Mandy back in the car, and went home empty handed. I've always wished that I was gifted with the art of drawing cartoons. Every time I think of this story I see Crickett in the driver's seat looking through the center of the steering wheel and a paw on each side. In the bubble coming out of her mouth would be the words "Finally! Now I can finally be the lone canine again. Stop moving so I can hit you!"

Mandy seemed to have a penchant for causing trouble in parking lots. My mom was visiting my brother in Florida, and so from time to time I would use her car. Here it was, a chilly, misty day. The weather was cool, so I took the kids because I knew I wouldn't be long. However, thanks to Mandy, what was supposed to be a half hour errand became two hours and counting. Perhaps some of you are familiar of the sort of locking mechanism this car had. Rather than a switch that could be flipped up and down much like a light switch, this one was flat on the arm of the door and closed and opened simply by rocking the switch back and forth. Normally I just take the cart to the car, but because it was drizzly I chose to drive the car to the front ramp. With keys in the ignition, I got out and walked around the front of the car—and that's when it happened. Someone passed by the car, which sent Mandy on a barking frenzy. I heard it right away: that click that tells you the car is now locked.

In her frantic excitement, Mandy had jumped into the front seat and bounced up and down non-stop, while at the same time barking her head off. Sadly her paw had landed right on the rocker switch and in less than a second it was done. There I stood with three grocery bags in my cart, looking at a locked car with two dogs inside and whose motor was running. I must say everyone did their best to help. People kept running back and forth beside the car trying to get her to repeat her maneuver and so unlock the car. No such luck was to be had. People tried to help me break in by sliding a wire down into the door to try to unlock the mechanism. Still nothing. By now. a full hour had gone by and the problem was no closer to being resolved. Just to add to the problem, it began to rain at a good steady pace. I was running out of ideas. Time to call a lock service, but the first ones I called all said they would be at least two more hours. Finally, I called the last number I found. A woman answered the phone and said her husband was on another job and it might take a while. I was on my last nerve and I cried "you don't understand! The car is running and my dogs are locked inside!" She immediately told me to hold on. Less than a minute later, she came back on the line and told me her husband was on the way. Two dogs locked in a car with the motor running clearly took priority. Just another reason why I love dog people, even if I did have to pay $65 for the service!

A new revelation for me was that as an interior house painter, my dogs supplied free labor. Just think about it. A short dog is the perfect height to paint baseboards with its tail. But even more importantly, my reputation as a skilled painter began to really spread once people started realized they were, thanks to my larger dog Mandy, getting a faux finish on their walls free of charge. On one particular job, Crickett went with me every day. These days most people used latex paint, but this was a very old house and any surface with a gloss finish was painted in oil paint. To abide by the customer's rules, I also had to use oil paint. The stairway to the second floor had a banister on the right side going up the steps. Attached to the hand rail were several posts, or newels, to help support and distribute the weight. I had just finished painting these lovely posts with a fresh coat of white semi-gloss oil paint and had moved on to another part of the house not giving the slightest thought about Crickett. I should have. An hour or so later, I went to find her to go home when I made a new observation. My little girl had morphed from dog to skunk. Without my seeing it as it happened, I drew my own conclusion. There really was only one right explanation. She had put her head through the posts and strained to see where I was. The result was a white stripe from her forehead almost to her tail. And don't forget it was oil paint. For almost a month, people saw me walking with what they probably thought was a skunk on steroids. For me, this was the closest I came to owning an exotic animal until I started owning parrots.

Stair posts weren't the only things my dogs left their mark on. One customer had a mentally challenged child who really loved being around dogs. Sounded good to me. Another chance to bring the kids to work. While my workers and I painted walls, the kids, both canine and human, were having a great time. It wasn't until I got home that I noticed anything strange. One of my kids didn't look quite right. There was a slight discoloration on one side of the torso. Wait a minute--the discoloration wasn't so slight. Her entire right side was a different color from the left. This is when I discovered the gift of free faux finishing. Mandy had dragged herself all the way across a wet wall. When I went to work the next day the customer just smiled and said "don't worry about it". Not only was there a design different from the rest of the wall, there was also a slight dog coat finish in the mix. In layman's terms: a faux finish with dog hair covering. If I could have trained Mandy to do that maneuver on demand, I would have gotten a lot more work!

Hannah the Cowardly Pit Bull

I fell in love with Hannah right away. We all know we aren't supposed to love one child more than the others, but we do. Come on and admit it. You know you have a favorite. As it is with human kids, so it is with pets. Of all of my dogs to date, Hannah is the one who stole everybody's heart. She was living three houses from me, and she was starving to death. The owner had another larger dog as well, and that dog was eating all of the food set out, which left Hannah with nothing. To make matters worse, she was not spayed, and the larger dog saw his chance when she went into her first heat. She soon gave birth to beautiful brindle puppies, which was odd, as both she and the father were white. She did have brindle spots, but we were all taken by surprise. She was a good mother and fed her puppies, but no one was feeding her. The pups were given away before they were weaned. At this point, a friend and I rescued her, by stealing her out of the yard. You could see every bone in her spine. She was in the ICU in the hospital for three days. Just for the record, that neighbor was pushed out of the neighborhood.

For a few hours a few times a week, I would visit her at my friend's house. Then a little longer and a little more often. After three months, I picked her up one day and she never went back. It was impossible not to love Hannah. She would dance when she was excited. When she ate, she would take a mouthful of kibble, come to where you were, drop it and eat each one while standing next to you. She would give the famous pit bull grin, dance, and then get more food to repeat the pattern. She was, without exception, the funniest and silliest dog I ever had the privilege of being owned by. Anyone who has had the pleasure of seeing a pit bull smile knows exactly what I'm talking about. The eyes shine, and the top lip raises to expose all teeth, upper and lower. An inexperienced dog person might think it the beginning of a sneer or an attack gesture. But those of us that are dog lovers know better. It is indeed one of the most endearing emotional expressions a dog can share. Everyone who met her immediately fell in love with her; they had no choice.

Hannah probably had more individual personality than any of my other dogs to that point combined. She was cute as hell, and dumb as dirt. Before you think I'm being cruel to the memory of my little girl let me explain. Hannah was, in some ways, well—limited. Take her reaction to squirrels. Seeing a squirrel at any distance would bring Hannah running at top speed, but my favorite memories are from right in my own back yard. No matter what the weather, she relished chasing a squirrel up a tree. Most dogs are into this hobby, but in keeping with her character, Hannah added a little twist. She would sit at the base of the tree patiently waiting for the squirrel to come back down. I'm not talking a few minutes here.

If it were left up to her, she would sit for hours regardless of the weather. Sleet, rain, blustery winds—it didn't matter to her. In the winter she reminded me of little kids at a swimming pool. They would be shivering and their lips would be turning blue, but they still didn't have the good sense to get out of the water. By now that squirrel was probably three blocks away, but Hannah would sit on the soaked or frozen ground, looking up hopefully, while she shivered hard enough to look like she had swallowed a vibrator. I had to go out and physically bring her in. I'd grab a towel I had warming in the dryer and wrap it around her, and it would sometimes take a half an hour for her to stop shivering.

Another interesting trait she had is when we would take her in the car. If I had to get something at the store and knew I would only be a few minutes, I'd take the dogs with me. As I walked away from the car, Hannah fixed her stare on the direction I was walking. If I came out of that store and entered another store in the same parking area, Hannah never picked up on it. She sat staring at the store I had originally gone into and never shifted her gaze. If I came back to the car from a different direction, it startled the heck out of her. You could almost read it in her eyes. She would whip around to look at me with eyes as big as saucers that seemed to be saying "How the heck did you get here?"

She did some strange things for others to see as well. We would be walking at the middle school with Hannah off leash, and several times we lost track of where she was.   I finally learned to look in not obvious places. She would run into a lacrosse net, completely open on one side. The problem is that she would just stand there looking at the netting. It never occurred to her to turn around and walk away. A favorite moment with our walking crowd was the time I was walking her on a long retractable leash. All was going well until I felt a tug and realized the leash had stretched to its limit. My assumption was that I would turn around and find Hannah going potty, and that's why she stopped. Wrong. She had walked directly in front of a tree and froze. She just stood there looking at this tree in front of her, having no idea whatsoever that all she needed to do was walk around it.

She was also unaware of her own limitations. One very hot and humid summer day, we were all at the middle school, walking slowly and giving the kids lots of water. Suddenly Hannah took off at top speed. No amount of yelling in the world could make her stop—but nature sure did. After three or four minutes she just dropped, as if all of her bones had melted. We quickly ran to her and I got her to stand up to walk back to the car, but she couldn't. Every time I stood her up she dropped again. Recognizing this as heat exhaustion, I needed to get her home quickly. My friend stayed with her while I ran to get the car. Fortunately, I live close to that school. It took both of us to load her into the car, and by some miracle I avoided a speeding ticket getting her home. I picked her up and immediately got her into the bathroom where I laid her on the cool floor. For at least ten minutes I kept putting cold wet washcloths and towels on her to cool her off. Within a half hour she recovered. That was just one of the many quirks about Hannah. I should have seen the connection right away—we are both slow learners. And she was a true creature of habit. She always followed the same path: around the long way to the kitchen and next to the lower kitchen cabinets. If someone was at the sink washing dishes, there was no choice but to back up when she passed. She was going to be next to those cabinets no matter who was in the way.

The older she got, the stranger she got. Somehow over the course of eleven years she went from "Velcro dog" to finding it offensive to be anywhere near me. When she first moved in she was very timid and afraid, had spent far too much time trying to stay alive, and was unaccustomed to affection. I just bided my time and waited. Slowly she began to feel more comfortable. Within a month or so she acted like a full member of a growing family. Crickett was still with us, Mandy was feeling very full of herself, and the bird collection was multiplying like, well, rabbits. She wasn't exactly coming into a subdued household. She loved sitting next to me. When I was sleeping she would climb onto the bed and mold herself against me, which saved on heating bills. Bit by bit she came into her own. It was a privilege to watch this amazing transformation. Even when we went to the middle school to walk with her friends, she stayed close by. Well, usually. There were a few times she ran off to explore but came back just when I was about to lose my voice from yelling for her. She made her own friends. Her favorite friend was a miniature poodle named Jake. As with so many dogs, when Hannah played she sounded like she was going to tear other dogs to pieces, which naturally made other doggie parents nervous. However, the other dogs always ran back for more. Jake's mother used to panic until she realized that if there were a real danger, Jake would have run away from Hannah instead of back to her. The loved each other. As with my other dogs, she went everywhere with me whenever possible.

So you can imagine my surprise when her pattern changed as she got older. She would be all curled up and happy on the sofa—until I sat down. At that point she would jump off of the sofa and go into the bedroom, which was the furthest point from where I was. If I went into the bedroom to work on the computer she would jump off of the bed and head back into the living room and jump up on the sofa. You can imagine what that did for my ego. Especially since her behavior was just the opposite where my partner Ira was concerned; she couldn't wait to sit next to him.

Winters here in Baltimore can be pretty frigid, especially in an open space like a football field. The wind can literally knock the breath out of you. After a long walk, all humans looked entirely too healthy with eyes that sparkle and nice red rosy cheeks. Most dogs are fine in cold weather; usually the colder the better. Human body temperatures seemed to plummet while doggie energy levels soared. That is—most dogs. With Hannah not so much. Fifty-five degree weather was colder than she liked, and so she had her own winter wardrobe. We started with just your basic doggie coat like most dogs can be seen wearing. It fits a dog like a shirt fits a person: arms through the sleeves and the coat covering the back and belly, about ¾ of the way to the tail.

We discovered very quickly that this just wasn't sufficient for Hannah. I really believe if she had the means, she would have been your basic snow bird wintering in Florida and only coming home in May. Unfortunately for her that wasn't possible, so we did the next best thing—we tried to keep her warm. This was no easy task. A friend of ours came up with what we thought was a good solution. She sewed pockets on each side of the coat, added snaps, and made rice packs that could be warmed in a microwave and then snapped into the pockets to add warmth. Well, we thought it was a good idea. But not good enough. Hannah still shivered with the cold. The next step was a full body suit for my baby. It covered everything: legs in back, arms in front, and a zipper the full length under her belly. The only exposed parts were the head, feet, and tail. Added to this to ensure the outfit was sufficient, was a balaclava. For those not familiar with this, it is pulled over the head and is pulled down the neck covering the head and ears leaving only the face exposed. We confidently went up to the school fully believing we had come up with a foolproof combination. Wrong! Not three minutes after getting out of the car, poor Hannah was shivering like a leaf. Back to the drawing board. Next we found a much heavier full body coat that was also wind resistant. It covered everything as well as being high onto the neck. Finally, came the wining touch. I bought a child's winter hat that had flaps that covered the ears and tied under the chin. Talk about a fashion statement! To everyone that saw her it was the most bizarre and motley thing they had ever seen. But it did the job better than any other solution. The end result was that Hannah had a more extensive winter wardrobe than I did.

Hannah was a nervous dog. Most dogs are afraid of thunder, fireworks, and other loud noises, but with comfort from their owners, they get through it. Not Hannah. There is a country club a mere five blocks away from my house. Every July 4th, they set off a beautiful display of fireworks. Where my other dogs shake and are a little nervous from the noise, Hannah would vibrate, and if not tended to would easily hyperventilate. There was only one solution. I had to sit with her with my hands holding her ear flaps down over her ears to block out the noise. Good idea, right? Not good enough. I had to get my mouth right up next to her head and sing to her until the fireworks finally stopped. Now that's what I call a special needs dog. The show of bad nerves didn't stop there.

One very cold day, I took her with me to the nursing home to visit my mother. She always loved to go with me. But on this day everything changed. She was fully decked out in her winter garb and feeling very happy; that is, until we walked through the main doors into the lobby. The receptionist took one look at her and started laughing her head off. Bad move—very bad. Hannah immediately started shaking, sat down, and refused to move another inch. That episode really stayed with her because from that day forward, regardless of clothing or lack of, I had to carry her back to see my mother, whenever she visited the nursing home. She refused to go any further than the receptionist's desk.

Hannah was the first of my dogs to show me how much she loved me in a very special way. Back to where I started. Hannah had only lived with me for a few months when she brought me her offering of what she deemed to be a treasure. It was night, the weather was warm but not hot, and the air was in a state of permanent mist. I had a dog door put in long ago, so my little friends could go in and out as they pleased. But this evening something different happened. Hannah didn't come back in through the door. Instead, she stood just outside of the door, scratching it to get my attention. And get it she did. She was dirt covered with traces of white showing through. Her tail was wagging non-stop, she was smiling her biggest happy smile, and kept turning around facing the other way and then back to me again. After she did this dance two or three more times, it occurred to me that she was trying to show me something. I followed her down the back steps and walked the few more steps to our tar-covered driveway. She looked down and then up at me and down and up at me, the entire time doing the happy dance. She was clearly thrilled and excited at bringing me this most precious gift...an opossum. I had never seen one in our yard before nor since, so it's a mystery where it came from, but there it was in all its glory. Now that's what I call love! The situation was too weird for me to be angry. There was nothing left for me to do but shake my head and laugh. I'd never seen her so happy with herself before or since.

Of course, this was one of those gifts that keep on giving—now I had to figure out what to do with it. So I called my trusty across the street neighbor, Ron. This wasn't the first time Ron had been called upon to help me with an animal problem. A year or so before, one of my parakeets flew down between two walls. There was only one solution. There we were, at eleven o'clock at night, taking apart the back plaster wall. I was happy I was able to retrieve my little bird. To show me her gratitude, she bit the hell out of me. Anyway, Ron and I stood in the dark misty air contemplating what to do with this...gift. Ugly though it was, I have too soft a heart for any animal in peril. We found a box and a shovel and placed the poor creature into the box, and we were soon on the way to a wildlife hospital. We both assumed the animal was dead until we heard a scratching noise behind us. Seems our opossum had been, well, playing opossum. We delivered said animal to the hospital tech, bade it farewell, and got back in the car to come home. Ron turned to me and only had two words to say: "that's two!" I understood it was time to go animal crisis free for as long as possible.

Enter Scout
Or
Did You Say You Work With Eunuchs?

Let me state right now at the beginning of this chapter: it is not possible to be more computer illiterate than I am. I mean it. On a scale of one to ten, I'm seriously in the minus column. You need to know this or you will think I'm making this story up. Ira and I were visiting another couple. We were having a very comfortable visit. Ira is an electrical engineer; David had worked at a fairly high level job with Social Security. As David and Ira got lost in technical talk, with Christina listening and enjoying, I occupied myself by playing with Mitzi, their German shepherd mix. I paid no attention whatsoever to the conversation. Why should I? I didn't understand a word. Suddenly David said something that really got my attention. He mentioned that he used to work with eunuchs. As I'm sure you can imagine, upon hearing this odd confession, my head snapped up like a Pez dispenser. What the????? I looked right at David and asked "Did you just say you worked with eunuchs?" For a few seconds everyone just looked at me with blank expressions—then they all broke into riotous laughter. I just sat there looking at them with absolutely no comprehension. One thing was clear. Either I had made a joke, or was the brunt of one. I just had no idea which. Now those of you who are computer savvy know he was referring to a computer system named UNIX. But it was news to me.

There were three possibilities that might explain this miscommunication. Possibility #1: I'm even more pathetic than most people when it comes to anything dealing with computers. Possibility #2: my ability to hear properly was greatly impaired from all of the live rock concerts I attended in my younger days. And then there was a third feasible possibility: my hearing was almost shot because of a beautiful ball of fluff and feathers that barely weighed a half pound. Personally, my vote would go for possibility # 1. But possibility #3 is not totally out of the question. My poor hearing has caused me to lose the thread of many a common conversation. Let me tell you when the major damage began...

About the same time, I bought my house, my sister and brother-in-law opened a pet grooming and supply store. They were within walking distance from me, and my four pawed companions and I frequently walked up to visit—and get free treats. Although it wasn't in the original scope of the business, they began to carry small birds such as parakeets, cockatiels, and finches. Unfortunately, due to severe allergies, my sister eventually could no longer be at the store. This was also around the time the big stores like Petsmart and Petco began to move into the area. As is usually the case when this happens, many small family owned businesses were forced to close their doors. My sister was able to relocate most of the birds into healthy situations, but a few remained unclaimed. Two were parakeets, also known as budgies. I knew nothing about birds at the time, but was willing to take the two budgies anyway and give it a try. Give it a try indeed!!! Before I knew it my life was overrun with feathers. But I'm getting ahead of myself.

I willingly brought these two little babies home. One was mostly white, while the other was yellow, green, and black. Both were beautiful. I named them Merlin and Arthur, after the characters in Camelot. The birds were sweet, but not so friendly, as they had never been handled. Hand taming them was a skill I would learn and put into practice for years to come. I had the cage, the seeds, the toys, and the water. But shortly, food began to run low. So off I went to a nearby pet store that had lots of bird supplies. Unknown to me, there were also a lot of parrots. Everywhere. Big ones, smaller ones, cute ones, beautifully colored ones. But I paid no attention to these side attractions because I was on a mission. I just wanted food. I had escaped the pitfalls and was on my way out of the store— and then it happened. I saw it out of the corner of my eye: a small ball of colorful fluff. I had never seen anything like it. All of the other parrots were yelling and screaming, but this one just sat quietly looking at me. I asked to hold her, and the instant I held her close, she began to make cooing sounds. Quiet. Soft. Sweet. There was no question—this bird was going to be mine. I asked the shop keeper if this was going to be a loud bird. She smiled at me and simply said "Well, she isn't loud in HERE." The way she said that should have been my first clue. Never trust a shop keeper.

Within a week, my new baby came home with me, much to the initial frustration of my mother, who was upset at my adopting yet another pet. Are you starting to see a pattern here? Perhaps the names Crickett and Mandy come to mind. I named the bird Scout, after a character from my very favorite book, To Kill a Mockingbird. I was sure it was a little boy, and immediately fell in love. Within the first 3 days I took him to the avian vet to make sure he was healthy. Since blood work was involved, I asked for a DNA test to learn the sex of my baby. Imagine my surprise when my vet excitedly told me that my new little baby boy was, indeed, a girl. But it didn't matter. I was head over heels in love. Scout was a sun conure. Very funny, very playful, and VERY loud! Any of you familiar with pet birds know that even a little budgie sitting on your shoulder and squawking can be very shrill. But compared to a conure, that noise is a drop in the bucket. When Scout was on my shoulder facing me and decided to share her observations by screaming directly in my ear—it literally caused pain. Honest. No exaggeration. Pain. The real deal. Several times a day. After weeks and months of this, you too would also be asking people to repeat themselves. I even began learning sign language, sure that in a matter of years my hearing would be permanently impaired. In the summer when the windows were open, you could hear her at the end of the block. Suffice it to say, everyone knew Scout.

Shortly after bringing my baby home, I discovered Avian Fashions, a company that made "flight suits" for birds. For all you bird lovers out there I can't recommend this idea enough. It was a beautiful find. It fit around her body, leaving her head, wings, tail, and feet free. It had a lanyard that acted as a leash, while the suit kept her secure and also acted as a little poop catcher. Once I had a few of those, Scout was rarely left at home. She went with me everywhere. She was well known in the bank, at the local carry-out, as well as in the neighborhood, because she often accompanied me while walking my dogs. And she could be very quiet unless she saw something she perceived as alarming. Like a balloon, a plane, other birds, or heaven forbid, if the Goodyear blimp should show up. That would cause her to put everyone on alert within a three square block area.

Scout became my constant companion. Of all of my pets, I really believe she was my soul mate. We went everywhere together. I owe my thanks to the wonderful retired military couple who started a business making and selling bird harnesses. I kid you not. She loved to sit on my shoulder in the car and make sure I knew where I was going. Even the cold weather didn't stop us. She would climb into the neck of my sweatshirt and from time to time just poke her head out to examine her surroundings. I can't tell you how many times I thought I was going to have to administer CPR, because I'd be in a store talking with someone when suddenly they would see this little feathered head emerge and look at them. She was with me so often that when I would go into the Rite-Aid, and when the pharmacist in the back of the store heard her greeting everyone, he or she would get on the intercom and welcome both of us into the store.

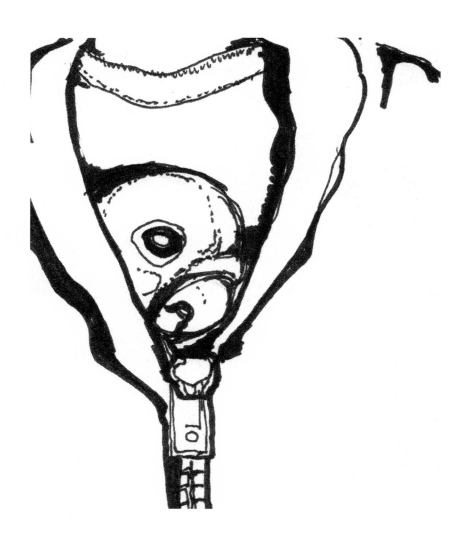

My favorite reactions were the ones I would get when we were out and she was sitting on my shoulder. If I had a dollar for every time someone asked me if she was a real bird, my house would be paid for. I mean, come on. Let's get real here. If I were walking around with a stuffed bird on my shoulder would you even want to talk to me?

At the time she came to live with me, I was taking grad school courses. I wanted a Masters in Biblical history. I was told that before I began any classes, I had to first take Biblical Hebrew. The only thought in my head was "why don't you just shoot me now instead of waiting?"" The Hebrew letters could have been hieroglyphics to me. Nothing but funny, squiggly lines on the paper. Fortunately, I had a professor who very quickly saw the problem and began working with me so I could move forward. Every time I came home from class, I went right to doing the assignment for fear of forgetting what I had just learned. There was Scout, sitting on my shoulder playing with the hair on the back of my neck. It was comforting. She was a one-person bird, and I was that person. We knew and understood each other. It was, I believe, the strongest bond I've ever had with a living creature outside of my species. She was funny, had temper tantrums, and went out of her way more than once to scare the hell out of me.

One big thing I learned from Scout is that, just like dogs, birds play games and have a great sense of humor. I had a large wicker basket full of toys sitting atop her cage. She loved to play hide and seek. She would raise her head out of the basket and call to me. As soon as I started in her direction she slid to the bottom of the basket. After I would turn around and walk away she would raise that little head again. This could go on for ten minutes or more, at which point she would go into her cage and glare at me...the signal for "I've had enough. Leave me alone." Even funnier, was how Scout acted when a stranger came to visit. At this point, I was living on the second floor of my house in an apartment. When someone she didn't know came into sight, she would puff up and yell and scream as loudly as possible. If the person turned around and left, she would pace back and forth, making what seemed like laughing sounds. She was very proud that she had forced the visitor to leave.

Like many of my other pets, Scout shared my good fortune of escaping disaster. She also shared my problems with being in trees. It was a warm, sunny fall day, and it was during the Jewish New Year. As usual, Scout was on my shoulder. I stopped to wish my friend Jimmy a happy new year when suddenly Scout was gone! The Velcro on her flight suit wasn't attached well, and when Jimmy gave me a hug, she saw her chance. The next thing I knew, she was in a tree at least twenty-five feet from the ground. I was terrified, and her constant yelling and calling to me told me she was too. I had no idea what to do. The people aware of the situation came running to the rescue. My friend's wife made calls to find out the best course of action. Someone provided a ladder and in a flash, I was as far up in the tree as I could get. Unfortunately, Scout was still a good ten feet above me. We brought her cage up to the yard hoping she would head to the familiar, but she was frozen with fear. We both were. This agonizing waiting game went on for hours. Someone or something must have been looking out for her, because the neighbor whose yard back up to the yard we were in, came to the fence to see what all the commotion was about. He did tree work and had all the necessary equipment. Do you believe it? Over he came, and up he climbed, to rescue my baby. Similar to the situation with Crickett when a friend found her, what were the odds of having a tree climber a mere twenty feet away? He approached her slowly, and she jumped on to his finger. He gently moved his hand lower and she jumped five feet on to my shoulder. I sat there up in the tree crying with relief. I repaid everyone for their kindness with batches of homemade brownies. For the rest of her life, when we were in the car and rode past that spot, Scout would scream as if to say, "Hey Mom, do you remember?"

Her good fortune didn't stop there. She was also on my shoulder the day my car got T-boned, throwing me into oncoming traffic. When I finally came back to my senses, I reached up and there she was, unharmed and still on my shoulder. People who saw the accident said she just fluttered up as far as the lanyard would go and then resettled on me. I may not have given birth to my pets, but we sure seemed to share an awful lot of life experiences and good fortune.

It was when I first got Scout that my food habits began to change. Shortly after bringing her home, someone sent me a link that showed conures from the day they hatch until they are fully fledged. Now I don't know how many of you out there are familiar with strictly kosher grocery stores. In the chicken department you see all pieces, sizes and shapes. And usually a hand full of missed feathers. They looked strangely identical to week four on the growth of a conure, when feathers are just appearing and breaking through. At that moment, I knew without question that I could never again in my life eat a piece of poultry. If I did, I would feel like a close relation of the Donner party. For those of you too young to have learned about this bold and ambitious family, they got lost trying to take a short cut to California to settle in newly developing land. They wound up fighting for survival through an unforgiving winter in Utah. Rumor has it that as the survivors were dying, they prolonged their lives by eating each other!

And so poultry took its place next to veal, a meat I had given up long ago because of the way the calves were raised. But all was still ok. There was a plethora of foods for me to choose from, and still enjoy a good night out with my buddies. And that was fine. I could have stopped there. But no such luck. Next came an innocent visit to a steak house. I'd always been a great lover of steak, and was really excited to order and dig in. I usually ate my meat medium. Pink but not bloody. But the person on my immediate left ordered his steak rare. One slice and all the red juices ran all over the plate. Uh-oh. There it was. That knot in my stomach that was beginning to become all too familiar. Suddenly, instead of seeing juice, I saw blood from a freshly killed animal. Down went the fork, tight went the stomach, and suddenly I knew I had indeed crossed another line. Steak had, with the blink of an eye, been removed from my daily menu.

Now obviously things were getting a little tense! Not to mention out of hand. I couldn't survive only on pasta! Surely there were still deli meats to enjoy. But even there, fate handed me a wrong turn. My ferocious pitbull, the one who protected me by peeing and running away, needed to take medication. And the only way (and believe me we tried many) to get her to take the pill was by wrapping it in roast beef. Again, no big deal. WRONG! Every time I peeled off a thin layer all I saw was sliced flesh. I could almost hear my insides whimper when I felt this door slam shut! So now, over a course of years and incidents out of my control, my menu has become very limited.

At least I still had fish to reach for. To save myself, I refused to have ANY pet fish, for fear of closing yet another door. But again, fate was out of my hands. Someone sent me a video of a diver who actually could stroke sharks until they fell asleep. OH NO! The killer of the waters was really a mild mannered, misunderstood animal with an unusually large appetite. And there it went, the closing of the final door to food reality. Out the window went sushi, and any fish that in any way resembled the creature from which it came. If I see the hint of a head or tail, I'm finished before I start. Suddenly, through a series of unsuspecting mishaps, I had finally crossed over to (oh, I cringe to say it) being a vegetarian. BUT NOT A VEGAN!!! I stopped short of running out of all possible options. My diet will always include cheese on my pizza.

From Scout to Harper

I am ashamed to say getting Harper started out as a mistake. Scout had just joined her friends over the rainbow bridge and I was distraught. I was truly inconsolable. I don't know what possessed me, but within a few days I made the decision to get another bird. There were many types I could have chosen from, but for some reason I insisted on another conure—this time a Jenday. For those of you with a little curiosity and time, I encourage you to look up Jenday conure. They are beautiful. The problem was that I had really jumped the gun on this decision. Not only did this *not* help fill the void or lessen the pain of losing Scout, it made it worse. Although she had the same out of the cage freedom as did all of my other birds, for a long time the only time she was handled was by friends that came by.

Like all conures, Harper is a clown. She came to me with a stronger sense of self than any bird I've known before or since. She has no loyalties, a trait she showed from day one. She goes to anyone, showing equal affection to all. Unlike Scout, this new little girl had a strong desire to explore. I very quickly learned to look carefully before taking a step; she would crawl down from her cage and walk wherever she chose. Immediately all unused electrical sockets were sealed off. Many was the time I would nod off on the sofa only to awaken to Harper staring me right in the face. She would walk over, climb up either the sofa itself or any piece of clothing hanging over the edge, and just stand there, barely two inches from my face, just daring me to open my eyes.

If I weren't afraid if it being chewed to pieces, I'd hang a sign in Harper's cage reading "Queen of the House." She may be willing to share her cage with all of her other feathered brothers and sisters, but she is not as accommodating when it comes to humans. She can shower me with kisses right up until I place her in her cage and then—watch out! If I put my hand in to get something or refill a water dish, she will fluff up and move like lightning. If I try to take one of the other birds out to put them in their own cages for the night, I am risking major bodily harm to any part of my exposed hand and arm. She is clear in the message she is sending, "Get the heck out of my cage!" Forget the fact that I am the one to provide room, board, meals, and cleaning services at no charge. This behavior cemented something I realized with my first birds that has held true to this day. Because their personalities are so individual and so large, I think of them as little dogs with feathers.

She also had some characteristics I've never seen in another bird. She whispers. If I start whispering, she will whisper back to me. I have no idea why; she came to me that way. I wish she would remember to whisper when she is on my shoulder facing my ear and has something very important to tell me. Better than that, she has her own avian version of the statue "The Thinker". She stands on one foot like a flamingo, tilts her head sideways so it is horizontal to the floor, and holds her head with her other foot. She sometimes stands like this for five or ten minutes. If I didn't know better, I would think she was carrying the weight of the world on her little feathered shoulders.

Here it is, five years later, and she still wanders at will. Ira and I like playing board games. Two of our favorites are chess and Trivial Pursuit. Personally I have no preference between the two—I'm going to lose either way. Whichever one we play, it is often a threesome. We will just be getting engrossed in the game when suddenly there is a strange sensation on a pant leg. We no longer need to look; we know who it is. Up comes Harper, insisting on being the referee and refusing to be left out.

In the last few years of her life, my mother lived in a nursing home. I kept her at home as long as possible, but unfortunately the money ran out, and I had to make an unpleasant choice. Fortunately, the home was less than a mile from my house, allowing me to visit often. I usually took my dogs with me. It was heartwarming to see so many faces light up when the furry kids came to visit. Never being willing to be left out, Harper also became a frequent visitor. One particular woman just loved Harper. I would put on the trusty flight suit and off we would go. When we got to the nursing home, she would strain her neck trying to push me forward so she could visit with her special friend. I would just hand Harper over, and they would visit sometimes for an hour or more. I would check in every ten minutes or so to make sure everything was going smoothly, and then just leave them to their conversations. What Harper was telling her I'll never know, but both the woman and my feathered baby would look at me funny when I came to take her home.

Just as Scout did, Harper travels with me extensively. Unlike Scout, however, Harper will go to anybody. She has no loyalties. Both Scout and Harper were constantly photographed. The demand came with the invention of a phone that could take pictures. Personally I hate being photographed, but these little babies seemed to assume being famous just came with the territory. Their pictures were taken either sitting on my finger while I held my hand as far away from me as I could, or someone else would hold them. A photographer owns a store next to the 7/11 convenience store nearby. Even he was enthralled with their beauty. He asked me if he could take shots of Scout. He took several and actually had one of them framed, and hung it on his wall for awhile. He told me people were coming in all the time and saying, "Hey, I know that bird!"

Harper may be the only conure in the house, but that doesn't stop her from having a love life. She became very attached to Sunny, one of my cockatiels. They spent most of the day together and he slept in her cage at night. She was very protective of him. In the morning when I would take him out of her cage to put him in his own for breakfast, she really showed her loyalty. She puffed up her feathers, opened her beak, and chased my hand all around until I was finally able to get him. Thanks to her, he believed he was very good looking bird; she spent huge chunks of the day preening him. Unfortunately, it wasn't reciprocal. Several times a week, I spent time preening her. As with all of my other pets it would never occur to her that things would be any different.

Early on I discovered how much birds like to take showers. Until I showed pictures of a typical shower in our house no one believed me. I first caught on when I noticed that Scout would always take a bath in her water dish every time I ran the vacuum cleaner. I came up with the idea of using glass pie plates filled with water set on top of all respective cages. All of the birds, especially the little ones, love it. Then I came across a better idea. I found someplace that sold pieces of PVC pipe with suction cups on each end to attach to the shower wall. I installed it, put Scout on it, and we proceeded to take a shower. Then it occurred to me that all of the birds would have a good time. Soon my conure and two cockatiels were standing on the bars attached to the walls, and the budgies were on the floor of the tub in a bottomless cage. When I turned the shower on they flapped around and looked like they were in birdie heaven. I don't think there is anything quite as absurd looking as a bird after a shower...soaking wet with feathers going in every possible direction. I've never seen them so happy indoors. I say indoors because I bought a kit that allowed me to attach two wire cages together to make one large cage for outside. I would cut branches with leaves and place them throughout the cage. The leaves provided shade and the branches provided climbing toys that could also be chewed. Talk about happy campers! They would stay outside for hours almost like kids at a carnival. It is without a doubt the closest I will ever come to creating what for them is a natural environment.

The Little Guys

I don't want to mislead you into thinking that only Scout brought out the avian lover in me. It all started with the parakeets I got from my sister's store. They, poor babies, were the birds that taught me how to be a good birdie mom. Arthur was my first casualty. I had no idea how easily new surroundings could frighten birds, especially birds that were never handled before. Poor Arthur couldn't take it, and became the first baby to be buried in my back yard. Heartbroken, I decided to try again. There were probably two dozen budgies in the bin at the pet store. Everyone kept pointing at a yellow one, but a sweet, blue, bird caught my eye. When I asked how to tell a male from a female I just stood there in disbelief. Believe it or not, what I was told is indeed the truth. The little section just above the beak is called the cere, and is home to two very small holes for breathing. The female cere is slightly pink or beige. The male cere—hold on—is blue.

It must have been kismet. I brought Matthew home and he immediately took to being handled, which of course left me feeling very full of myself. A feeling that didn't last long. Matthew spoiled me. On his second day, he was sitting on my lap chomping away at the baby carrot I was holding for him. I never ceased to be amazed that a living creature so very small can learn to trust another creature so large in comparison.

Scout had not yet entered the picture. Matthew and Merlin made a lovely couple. Alas, my new information told me Merlin was indeed a girl. I would walk around the house with one on each shoulder. As I walked, I kept repeating phrases hoping one of them would talk. I heard nothing for months. One Sunday morning, I was sitting reading the paper when I heard this squeaky little voice say, "Matthew's a GOOD boy!" I wasn't sure I had heard right, but sure enough he started say a string of words. That is how I found out that the males were the talkers—in our language. Unfortunately, Merlin was also a non-stop talker but only in bird-speak. She would chatter away with no break. For hours. One day she was chattering away when I actually saw Matthew sigh and just turn his whole body away from her. I believe that was bird sign language for "Please stop, I can't take it anymore." No wonder he was always so excited when I came to take him out of the cage. It was his only reprieve. And all that time I thought he was excited to see me. It just goes to show that even the smallest of living things can still do a number on one's ego.

After Matthew came a beautiful little boy named Sky. He was almost all white with a few small patches of blue. It was with this little boy that I came up with a method to help a new baby ease into a new environment while not feeling overwhelmed. For a few days I kept him alone in my bedroom. I went in several times a day to play with him and teach him how to "step up." At night, I would make sure the room was dark and (don't laugh at me) I would put on a CD of Kenny

Loggins lullaby songs. I kid you not. I used that method over many years. It always seemed to work. Sky was the first bird to scare the hell out of me. I came home from work one day and went into the bedroom to see him. There he was with his head stuck between the bars at the top of the cage, holding on to the side bars with all his might. I ran over and freed him and for a few minutes just held him close. It caused much more blood to quickly pump through my system than I wished. However, despite the mishap, Sky was my first success story. He lived until he was eleven—a long time for a parakeet.

Next in line was Snuggles. Again when I went to the bird store, there was a large bin of little babies. There was something unique about one little turquoise budgie—when I put my hand in the bin, he was the only one not to run away. As you can guess by now, he came home with me. When I took him to the vet for his checkup, I found out why he remained so calm. He was what we refer to as legally blind. He never ran because he never saw me coming! I called the store he came from to let them know. I couldn't believe it when the owner offered to take him back and give me another bird. I would never give any animal back because it was defective. If that were possible to do with humans, I'd have traded in half my family. He was always a sweet loving little boy. Not once did it occur to me that I might have made a mistake. He loved to play with his brothers and sisters, and had a good life for as long as he was with us.

Slowly the number of birdies grew, and at one point, I had twelve budgies at a time. At my highest count, adding in the cockatiels and conure, I had a total of fifteen birds. I'm pretty sure the reason my success record has been intact for so long is because of their diet. Every morning all of my birds (at the time of this writing there are nine budgies, two cockatiels, and one Jenday conure) get diced kale, sprouts, shredded carrots, little pieces of raw sweet potato and, when available, fresh fruit. At first this diet didn't go over so well, but just like kids, birds follow the creed of "monkey see, monkey do". As soon as one felt brave enough to try the new diet, the others followed. I also credit their environment. All wings are clipped so they can't get any height, but they can still glide to land gently. All of my birds are in the same area and all birds have the option of being out of the cage whenever they choose during the day. It isn't unusual for me to come home and find all of them visiting each other. They also have a lot of toys to play with, and once a year we buy a live ficus tree for them. They play in it, and eventually nibble the leaves off until there is nothing left but a skeleton of branches.

What I'm about to describe almost did me in. I had been out until late in the evening, and when I came home, it appeared as if I was missing five parakeets. I was frantic. I looked everywhere I could think of, and then I turned to places I hadn't thought of. Finally, I saw them. Do you believe it? Never having met Crickett, they were still keeping her spirit alive. There they were, deep inside the tree. Five pair of eyes just glaring at me. And to think some people don't believe in an afterlife. That was proof enough for me! I always love it when someone asks me if I have kids. At the highest count there were twelve little guys, two cockatiels, one conure, and two dogs. I loved watching the look on their faces when I'd answer their question "How many children do you have?" with "Oh, I have seventeen."

Make no mistake. Just like any animal or person, every bird has a personality all their own. For instance, my little keet Drew. In captivity, the average age for these birds is six to eight years. Drew is eight. For some reason, she found romance with Buddy, another keet, and began laying eggs. That's like being fifty-five and saying "OK Let's start having kids!" I mean, what the heck. If you just wait a little longer, Medicare will pay for it. Buddy became a family member after someone found him outside and knew I would take good care of him. The little guys had been together in the same group for years before things heated up. Now if she were an orthodox Jew or Catholic this might make sense; reproduction is at the top of their list. But then, according to my friend the nun, Drew can't be either of those. What is so odd, is that whenever she lays an egg, the next morning, I find it thrown out of the dish on to the floor of the cage. Now that's what I call maternal instinct—or a strange form of bird contraception. I'm just not sure which. I did learn a big lesson from this. Never bring a drifter into the house.

Roxie Steps In

After Mandy passed over the rainbow bridge, I could tell that Hannah was grieving and really feeling the loss of her older sister. I decided the best place for me to go was the city animal shelter. I should have known better. I don't know about anyone else reading this, but there is no way I can look at all of the dogs in a shelter and take only one, without being hit by waves of guilt. I actually took someone with me, and waited while she went in and came back with the dog that was in the most danger of not making it. Out she came with King, a huge black pit bull. He and I sat in the same small room and I spoke to him softly. No response. I spoke a little more loudly and in a more animated tone. No response. I had always prided myself on being able to win over even the most difficult of animals. I was clearly losing my touch. There was nothing left to do but wait him out, so that's what I did. I waited...and waited...and waited. After almost forty-five minutes I gave up. Never have I had a dog show no interest in me whatsoever. I was ready for fear, hesitation, anger, raucousness or anything else in between. But nothing? I didn't want to send my friend back in for another try, so my bruised ego and I got in the car and home we went. I had never gotten a dog from a shelter. They all came to me right off the street.

I knew it was just a matter of time before some little girl or boy would come my way. Sure enough, within a week's time the same friend who went with me to the shelter saw a post on a wall in the university where she taught. Poor little Roxie was desperate for a home. Her mother was in love with her, but the economy forced her to move in with someone who lived in a "no pet" condo. She had been looking for a new home for a few weeks. She thought she found one, but Roxie sat at the door and kept crying. The next day she was back home. I took the post home and called the number. The woman was thrilled. If a home wasn't found by the next day, the woman would be moving out and Roxie would be going to a shelter. Not good for a seven-year old dog. I met Roxie the next day at the middle school where a bunch of us walked our dogs. No doubt that all of the barking while the kids ran and played, was them yelling back and forth telling horrible lies about us. Roxie was a perfect fit. I knew the second I saw Roxie and her owner drive into the parking lot, that I was already connected with this dog. She was standing in the front seat, head out of the window, smiling while the wind blew through her beautiful coat. Before the car came to a full stop, I knew this little girl was mine.

As soon as Roxie was out of the car, she zoomed past me and headed straight to her new playmates. She showed her independence right away, running from one group of dogs to another, and then taking off on her own with a smile on her face and her tail in the air. I immediately told her owner I was sure that Roxie was a keeper. Silly me. I thought she would go back home for the night, allowing me to prepare for a new family member. The owner had a different plan. She was so happy to have found this little girl a new home, she brought everything out of her car and into my house. After a tearful goodbye, she kissed Roxie and left.

There we stood, Roxie and me, sizing each other up. There was an interesting look on her face. I would soon learn that, given her independent personality, the look was one of total indifference. Not once did she sit at the door waiting for her other mother. She had moved in lock, stock, and barrel. What really closed the deal was Roxie's physical appearance. I saw it immediately—she looked exactly like Crickett: same size, shape and markings. This same pattern of duplication would be repeated down the line when a dog named Nessa joined our family, but we're not there yet. The only difference was where Crickett had tan coloring on her face, Roxie was solid black. When she first came to live with us, I would take her with me when I visited my friends. I wanted to be sure she knew these were safe people. Without exception, everyone who met her was shocked to see an *almost* Crickett clone.

Later that evening, I found out what was living under that happy, independent front. I had always been accustomed to taking things out of my dogs' mouths, if required, from the day I got them, and so with total assurance I reached down to take a stick away from Roxie. She proved to be a dog of few wasted words or actions. She responded immediately and swiftly, by tearing right into my hand with no warning whatsoever—not even a growl or curled lip. Here we were together for the first time, and already she was showing she was the boss by disabling me. And then, just as smoothly, she went back to her stick. The entire event took less than three seconds; her execution was seamless. Out came the hydrogen peroxide and bandages. Within hours my hand was swollen. By the next morning I couldn't touch it. Off I went to the doctor to be given a tetanus shot (I've had enough of them for three people in my lifetime) and antibiotics. Thus ended the first 24 hours of my new life with Roxie. She went on to bite three other people before I could stop this behavior. For months, I would wait until she was chewing a bone or toy and gently but firmly hold her by the collar and lift her head so I could safely take away whatever was holding her interest without getting mauled. After I had it, I would wait about ten seconds and give it back to her. In time, she realized that she need not be food or toy aggressive. When people saw Roxie and Hannah together, they automatically tensed up at the sight of the pit bull. I should have gotten a sign for Hannah to wear that read, "You're afraid of the wrong dog."

From the beginning, it was clear that Roxie was at home and at peace with her new living arrangements. Within an hour of having her join the family, I took her and Hannah to the nursing home to visit my mother. My newest child proved to be the most well adjusted of any of my dogs to this point. Nothing fazed her. *Nothing.* I can't begin to know how much time this little girl spent on her own scavenging for food. I do know that she was very good at it. Of all my dogs, she was the only trash can diver. Of course like everything else in my life I learned this the hard way.

Hannah was very laid back when it came to food. She ate what she was given, never looking for more. Roxie, not so much. The first time I left for a few hours, it never crossed my mind to worry about what I might come home to. Imagine my surprise when I came home to find every thing that at one time was in the kitchen trashcan was now strewn all over the floor. I just marked it up to a reaction to her being left with Hannah for the first time, so the next time I went out, I still didn't give the possible consequences a thought. That is, until I got home. There it was again, trash all over the place. I thought that if I put a lid on the kitchen trashcan, it would deter her from exploring. Nope. It just presented more of a challenge, like a child taking great pride in figuring out a puzzle. Slowly I began to understand for the first time that with this dog, all trash had to be hidden away and inaccessible. I'm a slow learner, remember? I finally got it down to a routine that became a habit, leaving me with a false sense of security. I found that out the day I came home and she met me at the door with the remains of a popcorn bag around her neck. She had eaten through the bottom of the bag, and was wearing it like a Hawaiian lei.

Of all of Roxie's moves, one in particular remains my favorite. My bird cages are large, and open all day. Everybody visits everybody else. The paper at the bottom of the parakeet cage would often be in total disarray when I would come home from work. I couldn't imagine what in the world was going on. Much to my surprise I found out one day without ever suspecting the actual cause. I had locked the door behind me and started to the car. Suddenly I realized I left something important in the house. I turned heel and went back inside. Seems I came back a little too quickly. There was Roxie, standing dead still on the floor of the keet cage. She must have gone in there after I left, to eat any food they had dropped on the floor. She stood completely frozen. I had clearly come home too soon. Her only defense was to not move a muscle. I guess she thought if she didn't move, I wouldn't see her standing in there and then it couldn't possibly be her who caused the damage. It's a tossup between that and her meeting me at the door wearing a popcorn bag as her favorite 'you caught me' mistake.

She was no different outside. When we would go up to the school for our walks she would run to say hi to all of her friends and then disappear. I learned not to worry because she was always in the same place. You guessed it...the dumpster.

Roxie had another trick to throw in our direction, but she waited awhile to unveil it—she was an escape artist. Looking back, it made perfect sense. Her previous owner found her running around a very busy intersection. She was wearing tags at the time, and was taken to her original home. Upon seeing the condition of the home she ran away from, the woman took off the tags, kept the name, and gave her a new address.

I started getting calls from people in my neighborhood who were seeing Roxie wandering around. This happened three or four times. Finally, the idea occurred to me of catching her in the act. I left the house, drove around the block, parked four houses down the street, and watched and waited. Sure enough, along came Roxie, squeezing under the wire fence to escape the yard. It is still a mystery how she pulled this off. She was easily twice the size of the opening, but was obviously born with desire to manipulate situations to fit her liking. Fortunately, I have a very good neighbor who took it upon himself to solve the problem. He donated several pieces of very thick lumber and proceeded to staple the bottom of the fence to the wood, making any escape impossible. Roxie may have been frustrated, but at least when I was gone I always knew she was safe.

Let me interject right here that I never, through all the years, got really angry at the stunts and messes that belonged to my kids. I've no room to, considering some of the crazy things I did as a kid. My sister had a ceramic ashtray shaped and painted like a cupped hand. One day, I accidentally knocked the ashtray onto the floor, splintering it into pieces. There was only one thing to do; hide the evidence. Even at the tender age of six, I knew it was always better not to get caught. So hide the evidence I did, by flushing everything down the toilet. You can use your imagination to guess the outcome of that bright idea. I seemed to have a penchant for problems involving water. Although I have no memory of it, there were many times I was reminded of the story of the day I caused the dining room ceiling to drip water. My parents were sitting at the table conversing, when suddenly there was a drip. And then another. They looked up and saw the beginning of a small steady stream of water dropping from above. They raced upstairs and found the reason for the problem. There I was, standing in the shower—with an open umbrella. The floor was flooded. I was just singing away, oblivious to the problem. After they shut off the water and pulled me out of the shower, they asked what in the world I was doing. I simply told them I was singing in the rain. I have no memory of the event or their reaction. But both stories must have hit a nerve, because I heard them periodically for the rest of my parents' lives.

The Book of Nessa

Some dogs come into your life to keep you laughing. Some to test your patience. Some to teach you empathy. The main reason Nessa came into my life was to give me palpitations.

I want to tell you about Nessa, but I think it will help if I tell you more of how a lot of who I am actually all started—in childhood. My mother was what is now called overly protective, also known as a good Jewish mother. She constantly feared for my safety. When all of my friends were learning to roller skate, I was only allowed to use one skate. Honest, I'm not making this up. She figured as long as one foot wasn't on wheels, I'd have a better shot at staying upright. Obviously her way of thinking didn't hold true. I started out with only one foot on the ground, and have been off balance ever since. I have an amazing talent for being involved in horrendous accidents only to stand up and walk away unscathed. Rather than filling pages with all of the details of my past, I'll start with two major accidents within the past five years that show how I've so poignantly come face to face with the effects of my lopsided beginnings and still manage to remain intact.

The first time was when the scaffolding I was sitting on gave way. There I was, twelve feet up in the air, minding my own business and enjoying my favorite part of working as a painting contractor--plaster repair. There is great satisfaction to be gotten from looking at a hole going deep down to the lath work, knowing that upon completion no one will ever know a problem ever existed. It speaks to my need for instant results. The setting was in a stairwell that reached three stories high, with me sitting comfortably at the top and looking up while tending to the huge hole in the ceiling. Suddenly I got that split second feeling that something was amiss, and from the corner of my eye caught the almost imperceptible movement of ladder on wall. My last thought was "This can't be good." And so it wasn't. I flew five feet backwards and twelve feet down, landing on my back on a marble landing. My head missed the point of the step by less than one inch. The ladder went through a window. Pressure treated lumber landed on my face. I clearly blanked out, because upon coming to, my first sensation was that there surely must be a dent in the marble surface where my head landed.

I opened my eyes to many faces bent over close to my face, and had a flashback to being in a crib surrounded by grownups who just needed to take a peek. Being always responsible, my first words were "Don't worry...I have insurance!" How big the fall was didn't quite register, because what all the fuss was about escaped me. One woman in particular was intent on being sure I was oriented by asking me what my name was, what the date was, and who the president was. Unfortunately, at that time the president was not at all to my liking, a painful fact to be called on to remember at such a time. There was the sudden commotion of voices and clanking metal as the paramedics arrived. I was whisked off to the closest hospital trauma bay, where I was pumped with narcotics (obviously the highlight of the trip).

The doctors then proceeded to scan, examine, poke and prod to learn the extent of the damages. Just a quick side note to any doctors out there...it's one thing to remind a patient of how lucky/fortunate they have been. To continually remind them of what could have happened with phrases like "Do you know you should be dead? Do you know you should be paralyzed?" is a bit excessive. I was sent home three hours later, banged and very bruised, but no worse for wear. My niece, never one to miss an emergency, stayed with me until the first shift of a five day stretch of Nurse Bank nurses came to my aid. I was already friendly with the woman from Nurse Bank from using them for my mother. Now I was getting to know them on a first name basis for myself.

The following year I was in a car accident that sent me rolling out of the car and into oncoming traffic. After looking both ways several times, I began to pull out into the traffic while at the same time connecting my seat belt, only to once again feel that old familiar sense of uh-oh. You know the one— it lets you know something isn't quite right just precious seconds before anything can be stopped or reversed. From my left I sensed the image of something zooming toward the car, and once again had that feeling of "this can't be good." And once again—it wasn't. I remember hearing a loud bang. The next thing I knew, I was sitting on the curb talking with someone. Again I had been knocked unconscious. To this day I have no awareness or memory of standing up, or walking to the curb, sitting down and starting to converse. In no time I was surrounded by medics asking me if I was ok. Regardless of my insistence of being fine they wanted to whisk me away to be thoroughly examined, and they, of course won the argument.

First came the short ride in the ambulance, as we sped away to a secret rendezvous spot with a helicopter. That would prove to be my first, and if left up to me, my last ride in one of those. The sound inside is deafening; the woman kneeling over me would scream to me every few minutes to tell me how much longer it would be before the helicopter landed on the roof of shock trauma. Fortunately for all involved I was lying down for the trip. Heights terrify me; don't forget—I've been known to put a hole in the floor of planes trying to put on the brakes as they landed. Had the trip been made with me in an upright position, believe me there would not be enough drugs available to keep me calm and relaxed. After landing came more whisking as they zoomed me inside to once again be poked, prodded, and scanned. And just as before, the doctors all shook their heads in amazement as they gave me a forward ticket home. Now you need to know all of this to understand the most recent in a long string of incidents that gave me as many palpitations in five months as my other dogs had in their lifetimes thanks to Nessa.

I should have seen this coming. Nessa is a dead on copy of Mandy. She is the same size with the same exact markings.

The only difference is that where Mandy was solid in color, Nessa is a beautiful brindle. They differed not at all when it came to challenges.

Ira and I had concert tickets that we had been holding on to for 10 months. The event was originally scheduled for February but was postponed until September. It was his birthday present to me. Our seats were front row, dead center. And the icing on the cake was backstage passes to meet the artist. I prided myself on the fact that for an entire year I had remained vertical. As I pointed out earlier, this was no small feat for me. But I had done it. It was T minus two weeks and counting. I had taken Nessa to the dog park and as we were leaving I stopped in the parking lot to speak to some of the other puppy parents. That's when it happened. Nessa saw something, lunged for it, and without missing a beat I was face down in the parking lot. My glasses snapped in half at the bridge and fell off. I was bleeding from three different places and already had the beginning of a black eye. As I'm sure many of you know, any face or head wound looks like you're going to bleed to death. It's just the nature of the beast. Everyone around me panicked. They ran for towels, Kleenex, anything they could get their hands on. There I sat, calm as can be, bleeding profusely, and not making a move. While everyone ran in circles I just sat there, looking at Nessa and saying "My face? Now? Really? You couldn't go for an arm or a leg? You had to go for my face? Seriously?" I can't tell you how much cocoa butter I went through in the next two weeks. Fortunately, by the day of the concert, the wounds were barely visible. As it turns out I need not have worried. The artist needed reading glasses to see close. Vanity stopped her from wearing them, so she wouldn't have noticed any facial damage anyway.

I started with these stories because they have been the least heart pounding of the incidents involving Nessa. Her original name was Faith. It was a beautiful name, but it wouldn't work for me. Every time I called or spoke her name, I felt like I was mispronouncing the name Face. I wanted her name to be special; something that would fit her. I narrowed it down to two choices. One was Yaffit—a Hebrew name for little beauty. The other was Nessa—a Hebrew name for miracle. I liked one, Ira liked the other. We put it to a vote with all of our friends—you know which one won. Looking back, it was the perfect name for her. Her beginning was bad enough to make it a miracle that she survived at all. She arrived at the rescue emaciated, anemic, full of parasites, and heartworm positive. If all of that weren't bad enough, at one time something had been embedded in her neck so tightly her skin had separated four inches. Her entire neck literally had to be sewn back together.

Let me stop right here, and tell you about the wonderful rescue Nessa came from. The name is Noahs Arks Rescue in South Carolina. Please don't forget the letter "s" on arks or you will wind up on Mount Ararat. This is hands down the most amazing rescue I have ever come across. It is a last resort rescue; they only take dogs that are so sick or beat up they are going to be put down. Many have been used as bait, thrown out of cars, abandoned, or horribly abused. The people at this rescue literally give them their lives back. Unless a dog is saying "please let me go" this rescue stops at nothing, and I mean nothing, to give any dog they get a better life and find them a loving home. But back to Nessa.

Within the first five months that we had her, she repeatedly proved that the name Nessa was a good fit. She was sweet, funny, affectionate, and oblivious. We gave her a wonderful home, but from the beginning she showed a need to wander. The first hint was the day I got a phone call asking if I was missing a dog. Now please understand, before we adopted her, we had to send several pictures to the rescue we adopted her from. Pictures of the house inside and out, of the yard from every possible angle, and of the fence that enclosed the entire yard. It never occurred to us, after all of our dogs, that any of them could escape. So you can understand my surprise when I received the phone call. Was I missing a dog? "Not that I know of" was my answer. Then they asked my name, and wanted to know if I had a brindle dog. And still it wasn't sinking in. It couldn't be my dog. She was safe in a fenced in yard—or was she?

Finally, my brain thawed enough for reality to slip in. Something was very wrong. "Wait a minute. Is her name Nessa?" Why yes it was. Would I like to come get her? She was almost a block away and on a different street. Fortunately, along with oblivious, she is also friendly. I ran out to the yard—the empty yard. What the heck? I zoomed over to the house of the people who were keeping my little bundle safe. There she sat, happy as could be. They caught her because she was really friendly and came up to their dog. Somewhere in her little brain she must have murmured "oops." I say that because these wonderful people said they were watching her make her way up the street. She would go up on a porch, look around, and realize, "Hey, this isn't the right place." She went up and down the steps of every house on their side of the street until she came to their house. I brought her home and kept her in for the rest of the day.

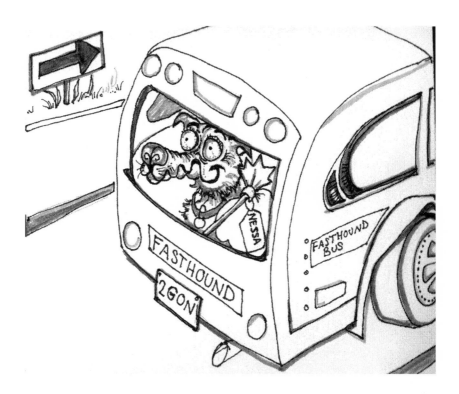

The next morning, Ira and I examined the yard hoping to see how she got out. We didn't have to wait long. As we stood at the fence, Nessa saw her chance and without a second thought sailed right over the four-foot high fence next to where we were standing. The solution? We threw up some lattice all along the top of the fence, and just to keep it foolproof, we attached chicken wire to the top of that. I had to stop Ira from making a sign for the front that read Canine Correctional Facility. The experience had been a little frightening, but she was safe and surely the worst was over. Not quite.

Her next trick left us close to unstrung. Suddenly she was gone again. What the heck? How in the world did she get out, after everything we had done? I called her name repeatedly. There wasn't a gap, not even an inch of space visible for her to make her escape. I called Ira at work right away. Our daughter was missing and I needed help. He quickly came up with a poster with a picture of Nessa on it, and the words "**PLEASE HELP ME FIND MY WAY HOME**" underneath. He posted the poster on our community online bulletin board. I contacted the rescue she came from. I knew theirs was the first name on the microchip and wanted to make sure they were aware of the situation should they receive a call from microchip central. I rode all around within a half mile area calling her name. The areas I didn't hit, Ira did. Six hours later we were no closer to finding our baby. I finally picked up my nephew Jacob to help me stick 'lost' signs everywhere. We stopped at my house just long enough for me to run in for more posters, and as I started to get back in the car I called Nessa's name one last time.

That's when we heard it. Faint—far away—but clearly audible. Jacob and I just looked at each other. "Did you hear that?" We both had. We walked into the yard, called her name, and heard it just a little louder. "Son of a...." I knew just where she was. I opened the door to the garage and there she stood, tail wagging like nothing had ever gone wrong. Somehow, she had gotten into the garage, and closed the door from the inside. If I had $100 for each time I had yelled her name in and around the yard earlier my mortgage would be paid off. And for all those times I yelled, she didn't make a peep. I quickly contacted the rescue to let them know all was well. "Did she come back into the yard the same way she got out?" they wanted to know. "Funny you should ask that question. Believe it or not, Nessa never actually left the yard." The response to me? "Thanks for the extra gray hair!" After this little escapade surely we thought we were safe. WRONG AGAIN!

Her next trick was so harrowing I came very close to needing CPR myself. Nessa came to us with little energy. Because of being heartworm positive when she arrived at the rescue, she was sedentary for a very long time. Bit by bit her stamina returned. After a few months she was able to run and play non-stop for an hour or more. That kind of energy needed an outlet, and that led us to the dog park. She took to it immediately. She was every dog's best friend, never meeting a dog she didn't want to play with.

There is something very special about dog people. Because their pets are social animals, so, by default, are they. Some people belong to a church group. We belong to a dog group. Everyone shares stories about their kids. They oversee their kids' interaction with the other kids. They get to know each other. In short, they also become part of a big happy family. As the weather got colder and the days shorter, a handful of us that lived near each other began meeting in our yards. One day my house; the next day someone else's. One day we were leaving the yard of one of the dog group. I had put Nessa in the car and was walking around to the driver's side when our little wanderer decided to take another tour. Before I got to the other side of the car she was out the window and running across an extremely busy street. Cars were coming from both directions. We all stood there horrified. It was like watching an Edgar Allan Poe story unfold in slow motion. "Miss Oblivious" paid no attention to the cars as they whizzed by her from both sides. She just galloped across the street without a care in the world, not looking left nor right. Someone or something was clearly looking out for her, because she made it across the street still in one piece. She ran right up on a porch of a house that had a German shepherd looking out of the picture window. I was right behind her. She may have barked, but I wouldn't know. At this point, my heart was pounding in my ears. I safely got her back into the car, with someone standing guard at each window to stop her from a repeat performance until I could get the windows up. I certainly didn't want to go through THAT again!

I thought I came up with a pretty good solution. I hooked her leash to the rear seat belt. Surely that would solve the problem. But it didn't. One morning on the way home from the dog park, I stopped and ran into one of those quick stop convenience stores to get the Powerball ticket I'm always sure will win. I got back in the car, put it in reverse, and backed up about six inches when I realized something just wasn't right. I looked in the back and noticed something missing: Nessa. Her leash was hanging out of the car window. I jumped out, ran around to the other side of the car, and there she was. Her feet were just touching the ground while she was doing her best to get back IN to the car. Clearly a move she was not used to since her big move had always been to get OUT of it. I unhooked her leash and put her back in the car. Seems I had forgotten one small detail. Unless there is a strong sudden tug on the seatbelt, it just stays loose. This allowed Nessa to once again jump out of the window. I was horrified when I realized that had I not caught the problem as quickly as I did the results could have been devastating.

As soon as I got home I searched the internet for answers to the problem, and found one. Ira and I hooked a bungee cord to one of the plastic hanger holders near the ceiling of the car, pulled it across the ceiling to the other side of the car, and tightly hooked it into the opposite hanger holder. Before we hooked it we slid it through the handle of a very short leash, which then attached to Nessa's' harness. This would allow her to lie down, and/or walk from side to side in the car. There was now no way she could even come close to leaping out of the window. I stopped to fill the gas tank. As I started to get back into the car I looked into the back to check on our ever so efficient system. Imagine my surprise to find Nessa standing there, tail wagging and eyes smiling, with one hook of the bungee no longer attached! The bungee hooks have since been reattached to the hanger holders...with Gorilla tape.

And just to prove that we had won the latest battle but still had not won the war, once we got into the house Nessa jumped up and in one quick move opened the heavy storm door. Before we knew it, there she was, racing down the steps and across the street to say hello to one of our neighbors. Fortunately we live on a very quiet street, or we may have had a repeat of her previous escapade. Now we live in a sealed world. The garage door is locked, the storm door has a dead bolt, and the car windows are fixed to only go but so far down. We think we have finally covered all the bases, but in reality we are quite aware it just gives us the illusion of being in control.

Not all time spent with Nessa is harrowing. We spend much more time laughing than we do tearing our hair out. I took Nessa and her sister Roxie to a friend's house to hang out and let our furry kids play. Our friends have a nice size sofa, and on the wall behind the sofa is a wall mirror that goes the full length of the sofa. Now I'm sure many of you have heard the rumor that dogs cannot see anything two dimensional. Don't believe it. Nessa jumped up on the sofa (despite the sharp plastic sofa protector on the seat) and suddenly saw herself for the first time. Some of you may be too young for this comparison, but for those who aren't, it was like watching Harpo Marx. Up, down, back and forth, ducking and weaving. No matter what she did, that mirror image followed her. It is the only time I've seen Nessa stymied.

Running a close second, is her reaction to outdoor Christmas lights, especially any shaped like an animal. If, while in the car, we drove past sheep, reindeer, or other animals, she would get excited and bark like crazy. She was in her best form when we drove to the top of my street. Someone had, among their array of lights, placed a lit up dog that was a little larger than Nessa. Every time she saw this dog she went on a barking frenzy. If window glass hadn't been so strong, there is no doubt in my mind she would have sailed right out of the car to get to that poor, inanimate dog. Whether it was to play with, or demolish it, is still up in the air.

Nessa isn't a big dog; she weighs forty-seven pounds. However, she has a jealous streak the size of a Great Dane. Allow me to explain. Nessa came to me very calm and is friendly with every dog she meets. Because she is so friendly, there has been a parade of her friends coming to visit. One in particular, a beautiful shepherd mix named Mitzi, comes for brief afternoon visits, and once a year stays with us for a month while her parents visit family in Germany. It's a beautiful thing to see. Mitzi is seven, but as soon as she walks in the door she turns into a puppy. Her energy level soars. She and Nessa immediately begin to play and wrestle. I think Mitzi thinks she is at camp for a month.

As often as possible when Mitzi visits, we go to the dog park where they have lots of friends to run and play with. I'm guessing the two biggest perks for her are being allowed on the sofa, and sleeping on the bed, which is not allowed at her owners' house. It's great that she feels so comfortable and Nessa loves having someone to play with. But a strange thing happens when Mitzi stays with us: Nessa becomes a lap dog. Normally Nessa likes the hugs, kisses, and petting. She sits at my feet or next to me on the sofa. As I type she is sitting next to me, waiting patiently for head scratches. All normal behavior. However, once Mitzi shows up for more than a few hours, something strange happens. Nessa becomes a forty-seven pound baby. At no other time does she do this, but suddenly she is sitting on my feet, on my lap, or on any part of me she can get to. On the one hand, it's very sweet that she does this to show her loyalty. On the other hand, I realize she has marked me as property that must be protected from other dogs. Never have I felt so special, and so used at the same time.

Sunny and Smokey
Better Known as Tweedledee and Tweedledum

I could be very wrong, but in my heart I truly believe I am the proud mother of the only bird on earth that needs a GPS. Had I given birth to him this would make perfect sense…anything in front of me is north.   My poor befuddled little cockatiel can't fly three feet without going in the wrong direction.

Sunny and Smokey are two rescued cockatiels that were acquired separately from each other. Their backgrounds were similar. Both were somewhere between twelve to fifteen years old—well into middle age for them. And neither was handled before coming to live with me. Getting Sunny to accept being handled took some time, but for Smokey it took almost two years. To tell you the truth, he still isn't crazy about me, but he knows the hand that feeds him, if you know what I mean.

Sunny must have an aura of romance. For some reason Harper has singled him out and marked him as her own. She spends many hours a day with him, preening his feathers. So much so that a small bald spot is starting to appear on the back of his head. He flits himself over to her cage every night for a sleep over. Fortunately, nothing goes on. They are different types of parrots and, unlike their furry dog friends, cannot reproduce outside the family. Every morning when I reach in the cage, he steps up on my finger and gets a free ride to his cage. Rest assured however, that Harper chooses her loyalties and goes right after me to impede the process. It's one of the few arguments I actually win. I guess it's just the male species in general. No matter how old they are, they are always still interested.

Now back to that GPS...When Smokey goes in the wrong direction, he usually does so by a matter of two rooms. My first clue that Smokey had a direction problem was the day I came home, and he was nowhere to be found. After a long search through the house, I finally found him in the bathroom, on the scale, weighing himself. I had no idea he was that vain! But did I catch on? No! Rather than limiting his access to different areas I still let him try to figure out the lay of the land. So far, I have found him in my hamper, in the closet, and on top of the computer console. It's sad. It's just so sad.

But I finally did figure it out and I closed off rooms by closing the doors, giving him limited areas to get lost in. Problem solved, right? Absolutely not. The icing on the cake was the day I came home and couldn't find him anywhere. I looked in all of the usual places—no Smokey. Had he migrated to his usual haunts, perhaps Harper's or Sunny's cage? No. Did he decide to spend the day feeling like a big man among the parakeets? No. Was he behind the sofa, one of his favorite hiding places? No. These no's were starting to add up and the total was getting scary.

Usually 10 minutes doesn't seem like a long time, but when you are searching for someone, it seems an eternity. That's how long it took: 10 minutes, and I finally found him. Anyone who has seen the movie *ET* will associate this. There he was, perched on top of a bookcase between a stuffed dragon and a stuffed wizard, not moving a feather.

From where I stood, I couldn't even tell if he was breathing. My only proof was that he was still standing up. Silly me; I thought only my dogs could give me gray hair. I've now added that space to all the usual places to look including the top of the window treatment, on the hat rack, on the kitchen table, under the kitchen table—well, you get the idea. Once he even went so far as to perch on the wires behind the television, completely out of sight. I've learned to check as many "he couldn't possibly be there" places as possible. And darned if he doesn't keep finding new ones.

Smokey has another strange personality trait. Cockatiels, like their cousin the Cockatoo, have what is referred to as a comb on the top of their head. When they get excited, the feathers on top of their heads stand up. When they are comfortable and relaxed, the feathers lay smoothly on their heads. Smokey is the exception to the rule. He must always be hyper alert, because the feathers on his head are always straight up. It reminds me of hair styles of the 1960s called beehives. The hair on the woman sat very tall indeed, and at least one can of hair spray per head was about right for keeping every little wisp of hair in place. I'm not quite sure where Smokey gets his hairspray from, but no doubt he must be using something. Often, even when he's asleep, I'll peek and those feathers are still straight up and ready for action.

Sunny is just as funny in his own way as Smokey. He often flies in the wrong direction, but not as far. He can always turn around and walk back to wherever he was originally headed.

Well, almost always. Every once in a while, he blows it. I've found him both on and under the kitchen table. Once I found him between the wall and the piece of furniture his cage is next to. Now *that* was a true treasure hunt.

Everyone has trouble refolding a map. I have trouble even following one. If I make a turn, I have to pull over and shift the map so it is pointing in the same direction as I'm driving. I openly admit that anything in front of me is north. I listen to the news and when the northeast is mentioned I look straight at Oregon. Many years back, a friend and I drove across the country. It was a fascinating and breathtaking trip. Breathtaking for two reasons. The first was seeing the magnificence of this beautiful country in which we live. The second reason was how long the trip took because I was put in charge of reading the map and giving directions to the driver. Big mistake. Huge! At least it gave us the chance to see parts of the states we weren't expecting to see. But for my friend, that was little consolation. Long after his patience ran out, he pulled over, reached out and grabbed the map using only three simple words: *"Give me that!"* I had tried to warn him, but some people just don't listen until they see proof.

Years later when I ran my own paint contracting business, customers would start giving me directions using phrases like "northwest corner" or "turn south at the light," I could have really used a good tape recorder so I could push the same button over and over with my voice asking "can you please break that down in left and right"? Sadly, even though birds can see a range far beyond anything we can see, signs with arrows painted on them don't seem to work. I just come home every day prepared for a game of hide and seek

I certainly understand the problems of travel on a very basic level. Some things are just hard to master. Direction is at the top of the list, but simple mechanics run a very close second. As I pointed out earlier, I went to college in the mountains of western Maryland. Why? Because I knew there would be tons of snow. It never crossed my mind to check out the curriculum. Because of this I went through several majors before settling on a double major of political science and sociology. But I digress. While in college, the love of my life taught me how to drive a stick shift. I loved it, but mastering those small details like being able to tell the clutch pedal from the gas proved to be a little problematic. At one point I was at an intersection where three roads converged. There was no light to follow, only stop signs. As I approached the opening it was clearly my turn to stop—which I did. The problem came when, getting ready for it to be my turn, I stepped on the clutch to get into the proper gear. Or so I thought. Unfortunately, I hit the gas instead. I lurched through the intersection as other cars were approaching. Fortunately, they had a better sense of where the brake was—three pedals can be confusing—and stopped in time to avoid a collision. Ira, not wanting to scare me or make me nervous, just sat next to me singing softly "Whenever I feel afraid, I hold my head erect..." Any musical buff will recognize the excerpt of "I Whistle a Happy Tune" from *The King and I.*

Speaking of Ira, He keeps a secret deeply hidden from the world: there have been times in his past when direction was a four letter word. When I was in college in the beautiful rolling hills of western Maryland, Ira used to visit every other weekend. One of these visits found us ambling around one night just taking in the snow covered landscape that brought me to Frostburg in the first place. It was late at night or early morning. I don't remember; either way it was really dark...and snowing. At some point we realized two minor problems at the same time. The first was that we were riding around with the gas gauge on "E." Many years before, my sister taught me that when driving a car, "E" does not stand for "enough." The second and more troubling problem was that we had no idea where we were. None whatsoever. Panic was starting to set in. No gas. Snow falling heavier by the minute. Finally, riding in a car propelled only by gas fumes, we saw a sign that said "Welcome to Maryland." There was a deep sound of elation from his throat. Then he showed his truly heroic side. He jumped out of the car, ran up to the sign, and kissed it. It wasn't until the next day when, safely back on campus, we discovered we were joy riding all through southern Pennsylvania.

Georgia

Georgia was a loving dog who was only with us for a short time but had a huge influence on our lives. She was sweet, gentle, and like my birds, had a difficult time figuring things out and getting them right. We have a dog door so my babies can go in and out to the yard as they please. Georgia figured out the dog door within the first 24 hours. Unfortunately, it took her almost six weeks to decide which side of the dog door was best for her pee and poop. She chose inside. Because of her difficulty in recognizing in from out, we had to rip a hole in our carpet. She always chose the same spot. Just as a side comment, I found it amusing that her favorite spot was right in front of the TV. The carpet was so bad we had to cut a 4 by 4 foot square hole out of it. The wooden floor was now stained black. It took lots of baking soda and elbow grease to bring the floor even close to the original color. After some experimenting, we found that a few good coatings of polyurethane seals the wood so there is no trace of odor. Thanks to Georgia, we learned the fine art of redecorating. While they may be out there, I personally have never seen wall to wall carpet with another decorated carpet right in the middle of the floor. It's definitely a conversation starter.

Georgia was also my first dog to love water. I often took her to work with me, and the highlight of her day was running back and forth jumping in and out of the baby pool. Nessa was the total opposite. Once I tried to put her in the small pool at the dog park. She almost broke my nose with her head with all of that flailing. Fortunately, she has very short hair and I can just take a wet wash cloth to bathe her.

There isn't a lot to write about Georgia because she was with us for such a short time. Several weeks after her arrival, she tested heartworm positive and headed back to the rescue to be treated and recover. There was also another problem that no one, not even the rescue, saw coming. The more comfortable she got the more aggressive she became toward humans. While that is certainly something I can relate to, it is not good to have an aggressive and unpredictable dog. We had no choice but to return her to the rescue. As events would have it, Dazzy came along to fill the space Georgia had occupied in our lives.

Dazzy

Had I paid attention over the years, I would have seen that not thinking things through is in my bloodline. Many times I've heard the story of my mother and her ice cube trays. Surely some of you must remember the days before icemakers were a standard part of a refrigerator. The story goes as follows. My mother was filling the metal trays with water from the kitchen sink. She then slowly and cautiously made her way down the basement steps to put the trays in the freezer. A friend was watching her do this, and asked my mother what in the world she was doing. You see, as in most basements, there was a laundry sink. My mom's friend pointed out that rather than performing the delicate ballet down the steps, perhaps it might be easier to just fill the trays downstairs. And what did my mother do with this revelation? She poured the water out of the tray she had so carefully carried down the steps down the drain of the basement sink, and then proceeded to refill the tray with water from the same basement sink! Crazy you say?

This craziness did not start with my mother. When my brother was in his very early teens, and I had just been born into a brand new world, we lived in a three room walk-up apartment on the fourth floor. These buildings were built in groups of three or four together, and there would be a six foot gap to the next group of buildings. One, day my brother and his friends decided the best use of their time was to bridge that gap by jumping from one roof to the other. Remember now, this is four stories in the air. My mother, looking up from the sidewalk, was horrified. My grandmother observed all of this from her window, and didn't hesitate for a second to swing into action. Did she call to the boys to come down using the steps inside of the building upon whose roof they were standing? Of course not. She threw open her window, stuck her head out and yelled "What do you think you're doing? You jump right back over here this instant!" What crazy things my grandmother's mother may have shown is unknown. But you must be seeing a pattern here. I tell you these things in the hope that I can fool you into believing that my history of ridiculous actions and decisions really wasn't my fault.

When I was in elementary school, someone told me that you could take a raw egg and turn it into a rubber bouncing egg, if the egg was left overnight covered in vinegar. The next morning when my mother came downstairs to make breakfast, she found a wonderful surprise. In the refrigerator, on the top shelf were rows of glasses, each containing a no longer viable egg. She came down to something similar several months later, when a schoolmate told me salad dressing could be made by mixing mayo and ketchup. I used every drop of both condiments we had in the house, as well as every glass I could reach to try this out. A few years later I was given a paint-by-numbers set. It contained several small cups with different color oil paints. I thought following numbers was cheating, so I painted an entire mural on my own—on the enamel surface of the kitchen sink. I guess now you can start to understand why my mother took a deep breath every day and said, "God give me strength." I was well into my teens before I learned it wasn't a Jewish prayer. For as long as I can remember, I've been curious about anything new, and caused my parents endless grief trying to reproduce every new thing I saw.

I tell you these stories for a reason. The only big difference between Dazzy and me is that she has more hair. Dazzy came to us from the same rescue as Nessa. The instant I saw her picture I knew we were kindred spirits. The minute I met her I knew I was right. Her eyes are always shining and dancing. Her tail is always up and wagging. To her every new day means hours of new adventures and discoveries. I thought she would take a little while to get the lay of the land—silly me. She came into the house and went right to work. Everything was new and exciting—*everything*! The floor, the furniture, the birds, the trash can. If she were a little taller she would be able to reach the kitchen sink, which would save me masses of money on dish washing liquid, not to mention electric bills from running the dish washer.

I fell in love with Dazzy the first time I saw her photo. She is a corgi/shepherd mix. We have no idea how that combination came to be. The only thing we can deduce is that it must have been the shepherd who had the puppies; a corgi would have exploded. She weighs forty-two pounds and looks a lot like a corgi on steroids. I was told to go slowly and be patient as she might take a while to feel comfortable. As we drove home from picking her up at the spot arranged to meet the transport, she put her head in my lap the whole way home. Less than ten minutes after entering her new home, she was running and playing with Nessa and Mitzi and having a blast. She is as sweet and affectionate as any dog can be. Her description said she got along fine with other dogs but didn't have a great love for kids. One friend who was paying attention wrote back "doesn't that sound an awful lot like you?" Indeed, that line could have summed up either one of us.

She has a true affinity for the birds. She never went after one to hurt them, but she couldn't take her eyes off of them. It was like watching a small child seeing bubbles for the first time—total concentration and amazement. She kept her distance, and for a very good reason. Because they had always been around dogs, my birds had no fear of them. Especially Harper. Get close enough to her and watch out for that beak. Dazzy may be many times larger, but Harper has no sense of size differences. She leans forward, the beak opens, and Lord help anyone or anything that doesn't get out of her way. Pretty heady for a bird that weighs less than a pound.

One of the first things I learned about Dazzy is that, much like I, she acts quickly and on impulse. And she is very shrewd at spotting opportunities. For years, Ira and I have settled into watching a movie while eating a meal placed on the coffee table in front of us. That has never been a problem with any of our kids—until Dazzy. You know that commercial where someone makes a wonderful snack and when they turn their back to put the condiments away, the food is quickly stolen from the plate? The person then turns around ready to savor the mouth-watering snack, only to find not even a crumb in sight. I made a much anticipated sandwich for dinner, and as always placed it on the coffee table. Realizing I had forgotten my beverage, I went into the kitchen to grab a soda. The time lapse was no more than 15 seconds, but as soon as I turned to head back to my food, I saw right away that I had been swindled. There sat Dazzy, licking her lips, eyes wide and happy, and her tail wagging like a pendulum. There was no question about it. She was letting me know in as many doggie ways as possible that she had just enjoyed one of the best meals she'd ever had.

What made this event a little concerning was its timing. You see, this happened during the Jewish holiday Passover. For those unfamiliar with the holiday and its customs, it is the celebration of the Pharaoh finally letting the Jewish slaves leave Egypt and head to freedom. It is the story of the exodus. It is a most beautiful holiday. It is bathed in wonderful traditions. It is hell on the digestive system. Because the slaves had to flee so quickly, so goes the story passed down through generations, there wasn't enough time for them to allow the bread they were baking to rise: Hence the invention of matzo, to represent the unleavened bread. Mind you it's not just the bread. For the duration of this eight-day holiday, we are not allowed to eat anything that rises. Therefore, all pastries, bread and cakes for the holiday are made without any leavening agents. The end result is that after even a few days the stomach can't help but rebel. Eat some matzo, add some cake, swallow liquid, and there you have it—cement sitting in your stomach.

Following this diet for the duration of the holiday, leads one to not need to eat again for days. The body has to find a way to send the contents of the intestines on its own exodus. I don't have to get more graphic do I? The way people deal with trying to prevent this uncomfortable situation is to eat lots of stewed fruit. Personally I can't put that stuff in my mouth—I have major texture issues. I certainly wasn't going to try to feed my dog this interesting little solution. Now imagine having a houseful of this food, and a dog that snatches any food left unattended without blinking an eye.I didn't catch on to what Dazzy was doing until the third day of Passover when I found a long trail of matzo crumbs. Sure enough, the holiday food had done its work. We lay together on the sofa watching movies; both of us with bulging stomachs. The result was a wonderful, if unusual, bonding experience.

I have come to believe the name Dazzy is a code name meaning "no matter how many times you tell me no I'm going to do it again anyway,", also known as "clueless but persistent". As mentioned before, she still hasn't learned to stay away from Harper's beak. That's just one item on a long list of things she refuses to figure out. I can say NO until I'm blue in the face and still, when I turn my back or leave the house, the same behavior will be repeated—repeatedly! No matter how tight the trashcan lid is on, the trash is always all across the floor. No matter how far out of reach, she will find a way to wrap her teeth around whatever it is I'm hiding. No matter how heavy the box, she will find a way to pull it off of a chair or table and empty its contents. I had a fresh bag of five challah rolls on the far end of the kitchen table against the wall. My little girl figured out how to move a chair, jump up and onto the table to reach her treasure, and then very calmly jumped back down to the floor at which point she tore the plastic bag and polished off those rolls.

A few days later we got a shipment of L-Bones for the kids to chew. The *very* heavy box was on a kitchen chair when I left the house. When I came home it was upside down on the floor with several sample bones all over the kitchen. She must have sampled at least seven bones before I got home, and I was gone for only twenty minutes. Even plastic storage bins with handles that snap shut, thus locking the lid, have been no deterrent. She figured out how to unlatch the handles. I came home to find her sitting on the floor amid at least twenty Milk Bones. Today, I came home to a true sight to behold. The entire carpet was covered with shells from a one-pound bag of pistachio nuts, plastic bag shredded and all. As if that weren't enough, she had eaten all that was left of bird treats. I think I know what happened. Mitzi was visiting for the day. Wanting to be the perfect hostess, Dazzy offered anything she could get her teeth on. Fortunately, I had hidden the corkscrew in a drawer. You're starting to see my problem, aren't you? No matter what I do or how hard I try to be in charge, I'm outsmarted at every turn.

Even more surprising was the day I came home and discovered Dazzy had a partner in crime—Nessa! All of this time I was blaming Dazzy for pulling the trash out of the can and spreading it across the kitchen floor. There sat Nessa with a piece of trash in her mouth. The look on her face knowing I caught her in the act was priceless.

Dazzy also has another unexpected gift. Of all of my dogs before or since, she is the only one who has the amazing ability to be fascinated by absolutely nothing. My car is a four door station wagon with a hatch-back. I keep the back seats folded back to allow maximum dog space. I will be riding along with my companions behind me when I will suddenly hear a strange noise from behind. The first time I heard it, I pulled over to see what this was all about. When I discovered the source, I just started laughing out loud. Dazzy was looking down at the area just in front of her feet, air snapping and dancing back and forth trying to catch—to tell you the truth I have no idea. Sometimes at home she will start staring at spots on the walls, the whole time jumping around and barking like crazy.

I know lots of dogs chase their tails, but this little girl gives it a whole new spin. The entire time she is chasing it she is snapping and barking. All still pretty common, right? However, she doesn't end by just falling down. She keeps going until she actually grabs a hold of her tail and, clueless as ever, yelps when she bites it. She is always surprised by this. It just makes me love her all the more because she reminds me of someone very close to me...myself!

Much like the rest of my family, including her sister Crickett, whom she never met, Dazzy also has a problem with hasty reactions. She and Nessa both came from the same rescue in South Carolina. Soon after Dazzy moved in, she saw her first snow. She loved it. That is, until she saw her first snowman. Remember Crickett and the ceramic cat? You would think they had been long related, because the reaction was the same. She stood there for a minute gazing and questioning, and then flew into a series of growls, barks, howls, and air snaps with her teeth doing her best to show this snow monster that she wasn't afraid. This went on for almost a full five minutes before she gave up, came zooming back to me, and for the rest of our time at the dog park, she never left my side.

Dazzy and Nessa seem to have some sort of unspoken contest at always being first in everything. They both race to the door to be the first one to greet me when I come home. It is not at all possible to show attention to one without having the other one right next to you demanding the same attention. My all time favorite vision of them is the two of them and the dog door. One day, for some still unknown reason, Dazzy and Nessa both made a mad dash for the dog door at the exact same time— from opposite sides of the door. Both of their front feet must have left the ground at the same time to push through to the other side of the door. Sadly, they never got that far. Nessa must have begun flying through the door just a mere second before Dazzy, because the door flap was opened outward. Both of them sailed into the dog door and promptly got stuck

Can you even begin to imagine how funny that looks from behind? Two dogs stuck in the door back to front. It took a long time for me to stop laughing and actually do something to relieve their distress. It was a delicate move. I had to make sure neither was injured while trying to free them, but success finally came. I have to tell you though, any tighter and I would have needed to use the 'old grease them with butter trick' to slide them out.

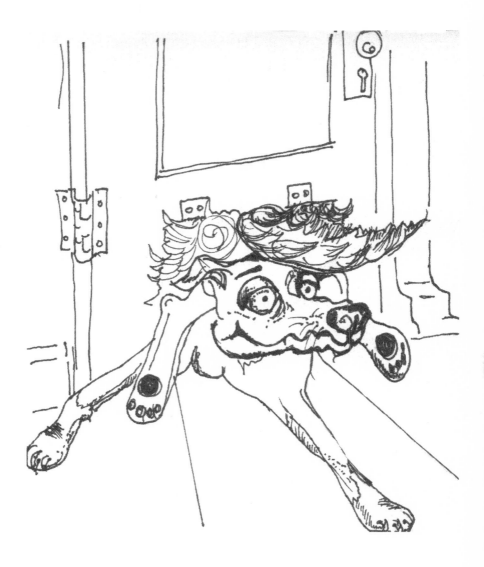

Things I've Learned From My Pets

It may seem like a strange place to start, but I'm going to begin by talking about fingers. My dogs taught me to value those wonderful digits that gracefully web tightly at the base and attach to the hand. We take for granted that they will always be there at our every beck and call. I certainly did, until dogs entered the picture. Often one or the other of my hands is out of commission due to an injury that can be traced back to canines; some injuries with a greater degree of separation than others. Take right now, for instance. A few-fingered typist in the best of times, I now can only use two fingers on my right hand: the pinkie and the thumb. Why you might ask? Well it's like this.

A few months ago I was opening up for the day at work. The entrance was closed with a large rolling metal door similar to those on many other store fronts. It has to be lifted until it rolls itself up and into the above containment slot. I tried with all my might but I couldn't get the door to go all the way up, so I got underneath and pushed with everything I had. I pushed with so much force I jammed my ring finger straight down and locked it at the knuckle. What does that have to do with dogs? Did I mention I work at a doggie day care? That's right—I get paid to play with dogs all day! But back to the story. Due to the nature of the injury, my finger bent down into a permanent bow because the tendon was damaged. Splints didn't work. After a month it was off to the hand clinic for professional help. The solution was to put a pin in my finger that reached from the tip down to the middle knuckle, the hope being that this would allow the tendon to heal. The pin stays embedded for six to eight weeks and was then removed.   Even though it was painful the hand was workable—that is it was until a week ago. I had taken my little darlings up to the dog park, and was in the process of adjusting Nessa's collar when several dogs came bounding up to say hello. Anyone who knows dog behavior knows this can quickly turn into a dangerous situation. A restrained dog in that position will feel threatened, and in no time war can break out, which it did. It's amazing how skilled and how stupid the same person can be at the same time.

Without thinking I tried to hold her by wrapping my arm around her neck. Sounds reasonable, but there is a major risk: the neck is just below the teeth. And sure enough, my hand came into contact with those very teeth. Like a really strong stapler, her teeth went right through the nails of the pointer and middle finger of the already injured hand. Believe it or not it, was good news that the nails were punctured. That way pressure from bleeding and bruising wouldn't build up behind a stationary nail. I suffered that effect once when my thumb endured being shut in a car door closing. It was excruciating until a doctor in the E.R. released the pressure by drilling a hole in the nail with a laser beam. The change was immediate. But now I had a much bigger problem. You see, I am, for now, in a permanent three finger salute. Were I younger, I'd make the perfect Girl Scout.

Now it is my good fortune to be ambidextrous. I can paint with both hands, I eat left-handed, and can use either hand to hammer, reach, or write in print. The only time I am right hand dominant is when I write in script. Common sense says that losing the use of three fingers should be no big inconvenience. Think again. I very quickly discovered how much of a problem it can be. Ever try opening a medicine bottle with only one hand? It isn't pretty. Especially since pharmacists, in all of their apparent wisdom, always put pain medication in safety cap bottles. Will someone please explain that reasoning to me? Of course that's where my ability to hammer with my left hand came in handy. Medicine bottles aren't the only problem. Ever try working with dogs with one good hand? The best I can do is put both of my hands together and pray that there aren't any disagreements among my furry friends.

My pets have taught me a great deal about human nature. It has been my observation that there are three kinds of people; those who love dogs, those who only like cats, and those who don't like animals at all. Let me point out the differences. There is something very different about dog people. Most dogs are very social, and so by default are their human companions. All one has to do is to go to a dog park to see that. The dogs run and play, pick their best friends, and generally have a very care-free good time. While the dogs are bonding with each other, so it is with the humans they belong to. It is not possible to be a dog custodian and not feel a special bond with other doggie parents. People step in. People support each other. It's a wonderfully unique bond that happens every day with dog people. To this day, I have friends I met through Crickett. The longest relationship is with Tony, the daddy of the fore mentioned boxer Georgia, Mandy's first playmate. I've also learned to trust a dog's intuition. More often than not, they can sense the bad guys before you can. There are no bones about it (sorry); dogs are clearly further up the ladder on this one.

Then there are people who *only* like cats. Let's be real—cats have a very distinct personality trait; they are born assuming they are going to be catered to. They are very independent thinkers, and so are their owners. Now don't get me wrong. I'm not talking about people who like both dogs and cats but choose to have cats. I'm talking about people who want nothing to do with any animal but cats. Like their pets, many of these people are not particularly social. The term warm fuzzy doesn't come to mind.

Finally, there are people who don't like animals at all. Have you ever met one? There is something very strange about them. They seem to be distancers, spending very little fun time with other people, and as far as I can tell their sense of humor is, well, very different from people who love animals.

Personally, I have no limits to my love for animals and trust them much more than I do many humans. I was asked once what I would do if there was a flood situation and both a person and a dog needed help. Naturally I said I would try to help both. Then the question became what if you could only help one. In that case I sure hope that human knows how to tread water. I've gotten many a dog walking job because when asked what my strong point is, I honestly say that I will do absolutely anything necessary for any living thing—that isn't human.

No domesticated pet has better hearing than a dog or cat, except perhaps a bird. I've had people tell me that birds actually have less acute hearing. I disagree. Harper can hear my car when I'm still a block from my house. By the time I turn into the driveway she is welcoming me in full force, and she makes sure anyone with open windows knows it. Dogs can be two floors away and will not respond no matter how loud you call their name. Just try opening a can or tearing open a bag of treats. Even from that distance, they will be at your feet before you even finish. Of all of my dogs, Mandy and Hannah had the most acute hearing. One Friday I knew I was going to be late coming home from work. I also knew a big storm was brewing, but had not yet started to appear. Just to be safe, I called home and spoke with Nancy, my mother's care giver. I asked her to call the dogs downstairs in case they got frightened. She replied, "What do you mean call them downstairs? Hannah is sitting on my foot shaking, and Mandy is hiding in the tub!"

In spite of their excellent hearing, no matter what you think, I can assure you that the following words hold no meaning to dogs at all: WAIT, STOP, GET BACK HERE, PUT THAT DOWN, DON'T ROLL IN THAT, ARE YOU CRAZY, KNOCK IT OFF, GIVE ME THAT, and #!XZ*^##!. I learned this lesson early on with Crickett and it has held true for every one of my dogs since. The following words have great meaning to dogs: RIDE, SNACK, LET'S GO OUT, SNACK, RIDE, SNACK, OUT, RIDE, SNACK. Sit comes with the original owner's manual. Any other command you can get them to follow is a feather in your cap, (no bird pun intended.)

I learned very early on that in spite of what non-believers think, animals can talk. Often people have asked me if Scout or Harper were talkers. For some reason, there is often an assumption that the only reason to have a bird is to teach it to talk. Not so. Their personalities can be endearing. Actually I think of them as little dogs with feathers. As far as the "talking" question goes, I'm relieved that they can't. If any of my birds began repeating things said in the house, I'd be in very deep trouble. They do, however converse with each other all day long. There is always the soft constant hum of chirping in the background. I had become so accustomed to it that I rarely noticed, but it was not unusual for me to be speaking on the phone with someone who didn't know me when suddenly they would stop in mid-sentence and ask "where are you?" To them I guess it sounded like I was outside in the woods.

The furry kids converse as well, sometimes non-verbally. With Dazzy all you have to do is utter the word "cat" and no matter where she is, the ears automatically go up. What my kids say to each other I'm too afraid to find out. For all I know everyone is talking about me behind my back. But they also learn how to speak to humans. I've learned to interpret many things from that low under-her-breath growl of Crickett, to the musical growl that turns into the full yodel of Dazzy. They have a way of communicating some things non-verbally as well. Often I will be at the dog park in the summer when one of my dogs will just sit next to me breathing hot breath on my neck. That's how I am told it's time to go home.

Understanding my pets was very easy for me. It takes some people a long while to learn their pet's signals, moods, and needs. I easily learned the meaning of every growl, whine, yelp, bark, chirp and squawk. I know the sounds for "let me out; let me in; I'm hungry; you're taking too long; pay attention to *me* and help!" Just from sound alone, I not only know the meanings but which animal it is without needing to look. In my opinion, the hardest thing on this earth to understand is human language. Especially anything hand-written.

Doctors of all kinds seem to be the biggest offenders. I've had my share of minor surgeries and major falls; enough so that I became quite versed in the art of translation. Let me give you an example.

I recently had minor surgery. When we got home and my eyes could again focus, we sat down to read the follow up *handwritten* instructions. They read as follows:

Reverse used ineduation Hydro 5/500 and eve poors on nuclear toy pens

Reverse used duck or talgate

Elevuth @ arm 72 hrs.

Keep inunison day

Mug revend are @ rewigs in 72 hr. newup fad too tipsy

Translation:

Resume usual medication Hydro 5/500 one every 4 hours as needed for pain

Resume usual diet as tolerated

Elevate r(ight) arm 72 hrs.

Keep incision dry

May remove ace and rewrap in 72 hrs. Rewrap if too tight

The way I see it, for anyone who can easily read the handwriting of a doctor, animal language should be a cake walk.

I've learned there is great truth in the adage "eat dessert first." All of my kids figured this out very quickly. When I set out all of the fresh vegetables for my feathered friends and add fresh melon or a grape to the mix, they go right for the sugar. Even my dogs picked up on this right away. I make food for my dogs from scratch. I'm sure that will set some eyes to rolling, but for me it seems like the better way to go. They get ground turkey, brown rice, mixed vegetables, fresh carrots, sweet potato and finely cut up kale. To make sure they are getting all nutrients I also include a dog biscuit. No matter how far down I bury it, the biscuit is the first thing to be eaten. I have, in all of my years, only found one exception to the rule—our shepherd friend Mitzi. She is, hands down, the most polite eater I've ever known. She takes small amounts of kibble at a time and actually chews them instead of inhaling them and swallowing them whole. Not only that, she always saves her bone for last. Unlike any other dog I know, Mitzi sets herself apart by showing a little class.

I've learned there really is something called dog park etiquette. Unless it is an absolute emergency, never put your hand on another person's dog to correct them. There is a good chance the dog will bite. Whether the dog bites you or its owner is sometimes a crap shoot, but more often than not someone will leave bleeding. Just as important, if there is a scuffle don't try to hold your own dog. In this case the likelihood of getting bitten is much higher, and more often the person your dog bites is you. Believe me, I know. I have the punctured hands to prove it. Always be on alert. Being knocked down can happen at any moment. Never be offended at picking up poop that doesn't belong to your dog. Sometimes an owner just doesn't catch their dog in the act. It is critical to keep the grounds clear, so when you do take that spill your biggest worry will be dirt and grass stains. No living thing, be it dog or human, wants to get into a car if either one is covered with poop.

If you have to talk about someone, test the water to make sure you are speaking to like minded people. Nothing is worse for dynamics to unknowingly unload on a spouse, partner, or best friend of the problem person. Never come to the park in good clothes. There is no guarantee greater that you will indeed need to purchase new clothes for dress or work. Finally, don't go if you are in a really bad mood. The magic of the dog park is watching the crazy antics of our canine companions and laughing our heads off.

Believe it or not, I've discovered there actually is a right way and a wrong way to fall down when hanging out with dogs. The wrong way is to be facing the dogs as their furry bodies are zooming towards you. You may see them, but believe me, they don't see you. If they did, they would not barrel towards you at top speed with no hope of quickly changing direction. In this case, your body will involuntarily tense up, causing great pain when those running bowling balls hit and you crash down like ten pins. The right way is to be mowed down from behind. That way you can't see what's coming, allowing your body to remain relaxed. You will still be wiped out, but chances are you will bounce right back up with little or no injury. Trust me on this. If anyone knows about the best ways to fall and get back up, it would be me.

Just because someone knows how to build a business and loves dogs, it is no indication that they know how to *manage* a business. My first job at a doggie day care taught me that. Contrary to what you may believe, the level of intelligence a person (or this case persons) has should not be considered a reflection that they know what they are doing. The good part of working with people so incompetent allows a very different appreciation when you move into a job where the waters are much smoother. I realize this complaint is common when working for any government department, but to see it in a smaller privately run company is just plain sad.

No matter how big or vicious your dogs might be, in an encounter with a raccoon, the raccoon is always going to win. I learned this lesson just recently. Early one evening I heard my kids sending out huge alarm barks. I went zooming outside to see what the problem was and was stopped dead in my tracks. There he was, sitting atop a six-foot wooden fence—the biggest raccoon I'd ever seen. Did he get startled? Did he run away? Nope. It was almost like he was sitting there sending out raccoon signals that said "You want me? Come get me!" I got the kids in the house and shut the door. Ira and I went out for a few hours, and assumed that after so long surely the critter must be gone. Wrong again. I opened the door, the kids ran out, and in less than thirty seconds I heard it. That sound all dog owners know that tells us somebody is after somebody, but we have no idea who might win. Let me tell you flat out--it's the raccoon. Again I had to grab Nessa and Dazzy and pull them inside. Nessa had a few small punctures that were defense wounds from the culprit's claw. A half hour later that sucker was still roaming around in our yard. We called animal control. They arrived within an hour, and that raccoon wandered our yard the entire time acting like he didn't have a care in the world. Right up until the time he heard the beeping of the animal control truck backing up. I've spoken to other people who have faced this problem, and all stories are the same. Barking, tossing things, water; it doesn't matter. Nothing will deter a raccoon—except, of course, beeping trucks.

Never yell at your pet bird. It is a complete waste of breath and energy. What I'm about to tell you is something I first learned from Scout, and the pattern continues with Harper. Birds have a crazy way of having fun...it's a game called "who can scream the loudest." They communicate with each other throughout the day with screams and chirps. It's how they say hello, good morning, where are you, come here, get away from me, and good night. Harper begins to yell the moment someone walks into the house. Actually she starts yelling when she hears someone on the porch. Even that's not quite true. She starts yelling when she hears my car in the driveway. When a visitor walks through the door her scream is non-stop. She is saying in no uncertain terms "Hey! Over here! I'm the one who really rules this loony bin!" There is only one way to make the noise stop. The visitor has to go over to wherever Harper is and sing to her. Honest. I'm not making this up. As soon as the singing begins she starts dancing. It's a riot to watch. She sways and bobs her head in time to the singing. There is, however, one rule...she needs to hear her name incorporated into the lyrics. Whenever she hears her name she yells. Loudly. Once she feels that she has been the center of attention, she quiets down. Screaming at a bird is considered an invitation to scream along. There's no getting around it; the effort is futile. There is a direct correlation between how often a bird is yelled at and the level of hearing loss the owner suffers. It's easy to assume that hearing loss would lead to a less painful experience when the bird yells. Not so. The noise isn't called piercing for nothing.

A clean home/car and a happy home/car are not the same thing. I have birds and dogs. This means I also have fur and feathers. Everywhere. On the floor, the furniture, on the bed. I always know a happy car when I see one. I can tell by the number of nose smudges on the windows. I can spend my time at home doing one of two things. I can either play with or entertain my kids, or I can be diligent and clean every single day. I always choose the former, especially if it's muddy outside. I have a dog door that is always accessible, which means my kids go in and out all day long. It also means that, on a muddy day, the mud from their feet as they run in and out can collect enough dirt to build small hills in the kitchen. Looking down at the floor, it's like looking at a topical map of the Rockies. Sometimes it seems pointless to do anything since within one hour of cleaning, the fur and feathers have already started to once again take over. One major cleaning once a week works for me. If someone doesn't like fur and feathers, it's probably best they don't attempt to get comfortable in my house.

I have learned that size and bravery do not go hand in hand. Mitzi is a shepherd mix who is an honorary member of our family. She comes to play with Nessa and Dazzy a few days a week. One month every winter, she stays here while her parents go to Germany. When she is here, I think she thinks she is at camp. She jumps up to lie on the sofa. She sleeps on my bed. She runs in and out through the dog door. Out of all three dogs, Mitzi outweighs my biggest, Nessa, by at least twenty pounds. Mitzi also happens to have what is, at least in comparison to my dogs, an unusual fear of wind. Not being out in it, just hearing it. We have had a blustery winter while she was visiting here. I have spent many a night with a 75-pound vibrating dog on my lap. Mitzi and I go into the living room, I put the television on low, and I try to find something to watch to aid my staying awake with her. It wouldn't be so bad if she didn't sit on my lap. Ever try to watch TV around a dog that size? It isn't easy. We are just ending a 48 hour stretch of major wind storms. We are both sitting comfortably on the sofa. We are both taking Xanax.

The most important thing I learned from my furry and feathered kids is the abundance of love that someone can feel for another living thing. Thanks to them, I have learned patience, and perseverance. I have learned that little things sometimes make you laugh the hardest. I've learned to be selfless enough to let them go rather than allow them to suffer, and I've experienced the deep pain of losing a life so precious to my world. The bottom line is that I am a better person because they allowed me to share their lives. What could possibly be better than that?

End Notes

Some chapters are longer than others. This is not because I loved one pet more than another. The length of each chapter is proportional to how long each pet stayed and shared their life with me.

Rest assured all of my pets lived life to the fullest. I don't speak of any pet's demise because I would rather focus only on the happy times. We've all had enough hard times to live with.

The answer to the puzzle of why I was not allowed to have pets finally became clear. My mother loved animals, but was afraid to get attached to them. Good-byes are harder for some than others.

Acknowledgments

My sincere thanks to all of the people who helped make this book possible:

To Ira, who stood by me with encouragement from day one. To Judy for her continued patience as I walked through this process. To Beth, Dana, Diane, Margie and Tony who all worked to keep me glued together, making sure I could reach my goal.

Special thanks to: Jim Yannatelli for not only allowing me to take the time to complete my project, but also making sure I still had a job to come back to; to Diane Schneider, who so generously donated her time and knowledge as a librarian to help steer my stories in a better direction, and to Melanie Fried, who so wonderfully captured the personalities of all of my furry and feathered kids in her amazing illustrations.

And, of course, Sarah B.